I'M NOT
HANGING NOODLES
ON YOUR EARS

· · · ·

and other
INTRIGUING IDIOMS
from around the world

· · · ·

JAG BHALLA
with drawings by
JULIA SUITS

NATIONAL GEOGRAPHIC

WASHINGTON, D.C.

Published by the National Geographic Society
1145 17th Street N.W., Washington, D.C. 20036

ISBN: 978-1-4262-0458-6

The National Geographic Society is one of the world's largest nonprofit scientific and educational organizations. Founded in 1888 to "increase and diffuse geographic knowledge," the Society works to inspire people to care about the planet. It reaches more than 325 million people worldwide each month through its oficial journal, NATIONAL GEOGRAPHIC, and other magazines; National Geographic Channel; television documentaries; music; radio; films; books; DVDs; maps; exhibitions; school publishing programs; interactive media; and merchandise. National Geographic has funded more than 9,000 scientific research, conservation and exploration projects and supports an education program combating geographic illiteracy. For more information, visit nationalgeographic.com.

For more information, please call 1-800-NGS LINE
(647-5463) or write to the following address:

National Geographic Society
1145 17th Street N.W.
Washington, D.C. 20036-4688 U.S.A.

Visit us online at www.nationalgeographic.com/books

For information about special discounts for bulk purchases,
please contact National Geographic Books Special Sales: ngspecsales@ngs.org

For rights or permissions inquiries, please contact
National Geographic Books Subsidiary Rights: ngbookrights@ngs.org

Printed in the U.S.A.

Interior design by Melissa Farris.

13/RRDC-CML/3

CONTENTS

In memory of my beloved parents,
Bachan Singh Bhalla MBE and Tripta Bhalla

To bang your butt on the ground
French: to die laughing

THIS BOOK CAN SAVE YOU DECADES OF EFFORT!

I'm not hanging noodles on your ears!

THIS BOOK IS DESIGNED to fit into our attention-deficit-disorder-ly lifestyles. I've tried to focus on the fact that we all have much else that we are struggling to keep in mind. So this horde of plundered international idioms is intended for low-commitment sampling and easy reading. The main attractions can be enjoyed, in any order and without any preliminary reading. This introductory text is not essential. Nor are the introductory texts of the chapters that follow. Some readers might benefit from the overview "On Idiom Technicalities." But don't feel obligated; in fact, feel free to *cut to the chase* and to start discovering the joys of randomly diving into the idiom lists (seren-dipping).

On the Origin of This Book

I love language. Sadly that's not plural. I'm essentially monolingual. That's what led me to write (or, more accurately, compile) this book. I marvel at the joys of the one language I'm fluent in. Stumbling upon a new word, a surprising construct, or a well-sculpted phrase can be thrilling. I'm constantly reminded of how important language is to the way we see the world. Languages give their users different lenses through which to view their respective corners of the world. I've always worried that I'm missing out on a whole world's worth of linguistic riches. I've always been envious (or, as they say in Hindi, "had a snake writhing in my intestines" or, in Japanese, "burned grilled rice cakes") of those whose vision isn't limited to a single language. And that includes the more than three-quarters of humanity that is at least bilingual. I've always been envious (or "rolled on thorns" in Hindi) of the sophisticated illuminating anecdotes that well-traveled multilinguals throw around at cocktail parties. And my worry and envy haven't all been for naught.

Monolinguals' brains are less well exercised than those of bilinguals. On average, lifelong bilinguals get Alzheimer's four years later.[1] Neuroscientists think that being bilingual builds mind "muscle" (or, to use the technical lingo, "cognitive reserve"). And having brawnier brains protects against dementia. Seriously, *I'm not pulling your leg* (or, as the Russians say, "I'm not hanging noodles on your ears").

Even if there weren't a potential mental health benefit, I'd love to be able to revel in the world's linguistic treasure trove. Unfortunately, I don't have an aptitude for languages. Technically speaking, I've lost that aptitude, since all healthy babies are born with the remarkable ability to effortlessly learn any of the world's languages. Nor do I have the time, energy, or discipline to spend years learning even one or two more languages. Put another, more accurate way, I'm too lazy (or, as the French say, "I have a hair in my hand" or "I'm a codfish," or, according to the Japanese, "I smell of things").

Is there an easy way to be a lazy armchair polyglot? Of course there is! Talented and dedicated explorers have ventured to the *four corners of the world* ("eight corners" in Hindi) and returned with souvenir collections of linguistic gems. The books recording their adventures can be easily acquired and read in an armchair near you. No visas, immunizations, or actual travel required.

Two of the best such books are Howard Rheingold's *They Have a Word for It* (sadly now out of print) and Adam Jacot de Boinod's *The Meaning of Tingo*. Both collect words and ideas from other languages that have no direct translation into English. Rheingold goes into some depth for a scholarly and fun selection from 20 or so languages. Jacot de Boinod doesn't go into as much detail but amazingly and very entertainingly covers 120 languages. For example, he reports that Germans have a single word that means the "disappointment one feels when something turns out not nearly as badly as one had expected." Something about that just seems quintessentially German. Another wonderful example that comes from one of my peoples is a two-word Hindi expression that means: a person so miserly that if a fly fell into his cup of tea, he would fish it out and suck it dry before throwing it away. Truly marvelous!

In addition to untranslatable words, those books contain a smattering of idioms, like the Russian "I'm not hanging noodles on your ears." Idioms are colorful and curious expressions that have always fascinated me. The technical definition of an idiom is a group of words always used together as a phrase, where the meaning of the phrase isn't clear from the meaning of the words in it, e.g., *he kicked the bucket* (or, in French, "he passed his weapon to the left" or "she swallowed her birth certificate"). Idioms are in a sense untranslatable even in their own languages. They are pre-solved little cryptic word puzzles.

The search for a collection of entertaining international idioms proved disappointing, though there are many books that cover idioms for use in learning a particular language. *Idiom's Delight* by Sue Brock (also sadly out of print) was the closest thing out there. It's a witty collection of idioms from four related Romance languages ... but it still didn't quite *hit the spot*.

Thus I set about filling the gap. Given my already confessed deficiencies, I've had to rely on dictionaries that include idioms and literal English translations (or in a couple of instances, on hiring translators). Herein are more than 1,000 amusing and thought-tickling idioms from several languages: Italian, French, Spanish (including several Latin American versions), Japanese, Russian, German, Chinese (Mandarin), and Hindi, with a smattering of Hebrew and Arabic, as well as fleeting guest appearances from others. These I've loosely organized by theme. Also, I haven't been too *nit picky* (or, as the Italians say, "looked for hairs inside an egg" or, according to the Japanese, "made the outside corners of my eyes stand up"). I've included expressions that might strain the technical definition of an idiom, such as amusing proverbs, phrases, or words that were simply irresistible.

On the Uses of This Book

Clinical trials to support possible therapeutic claims for this book are underway, but it's too early to know if reading it can delay the onset of dementia. Initial results indicate that it might at least be an entertaining diversion (or, as the Italians would say, "a thought expeller"). I hope it might also help you see the world a little differently, through the eyes and word images of other cultures.

The recommended dose is a few pages at a time. Beyond that, there is a small danger that the idioms in this book might cause you *to die laughing* (or, as the Japanese might say, to "get your jaw dislocated" or the Spanish "to be as peeled as a banana"). Assuming you are prepared to take that risk—this book is guaranteed to help you avoid having to spend decades mastering the subtleties of multiple languages. ...

If you already are fluent in all of these languages, however, this would be a nice gift for your less accomplished friends, acquaintances, colleagues ... etc.

On Idiom Technicalities

As I've mentioned, the definition of an idiom is a group of words that are used as a single unit, the meaning of which is not clear from the meanings of the constituent words. To a linguist, idioms and words are both *lexemes.* They are self-contained units for conveying meaning. Words themselves are often compounded from simpler words (e.g., scarecrow) or from other smaller meaningful elements, called *morphemes.* Their study is called *morphology.* The word morphology itself provides an excellent example of morphemes at work. You know that *ology* means the study of whatever it's appended to, even though "ology" isn't a word *in its own right.* It's a morpheme. Combinations of morphemes are responsible for creating and conveying the meanings of many words—a sort of lexical-Lego.*

Idioms add further layers of complexity; words made of morphemes are strung together in a phrase that follows normal syntax and grammar rules—plus the further

---

* *Lexical-Lego can be taken to extremes. For example, David Crystal in* Words, Words, Words *reports on a word that means "fear of long words" (hyphenated for ease of decryption):* hippopoto-monstro-sesquippedalio-phobia—*that's 36 letters!*

twist that the words just don't add up. In idiom-ology, two plus two isn't four, and often isn't even close to four. An idiom's compound meaning is not the sum of the meanings of its parts. That makes idiom comprehension an interesting exercise. As you hear or read an idiom, at some point you have to make a switch from understanding the individual words in sequence to interpreting the phrase as a whole and then substituting the non-literal meaning. That's a complex cognitive activity—one usually mastered only by speakers with a very high degree of fluency. Clearly, using idioms isn't the most efficient way of getting one's point across. Why say "he kicked the bucket," which has five syllables, when you could say "he died," which has just two? No one knows ... but interestingly, despite this inefficiency, we often prefer to use idioms. We use them significantly more frequently while speaking than in text. Perhaps it's preferable for us, in other ways, to rely on these well-worn grooves of thought and expression.

Idioms are related to metaphors, similes, and other figures of speech, and to slang, proverbs, aphorisms, jokes, and other forms of non-literal language. All known cultures use non-literal language. One way to think of some idioms is that they are fossilized metaphors. Their meanings were probably quite clear when they were coined and gained wide currency, but their use continued, even after the direct connection was lost. For example, *letting the cat out of the bag* originally referred to a way of avoiding the common fraud in 16th-century markets of selling a cheap substitute—a cat hidden in a bag, instead of a pricier piglet. Similar expressions exist in Spanish "to sell cat for rabbit" and Germans "to buy a cat in a bag."

The word idiom has the same root as *idio*syncratic and *idiot*: *idios,* Greek for "of one's own" or "private." The original meaning of "idiot" was someone who was not interested in public affairs (considered a key duty in ancient Greece*). Similarly, idioms are a form of private expression, private to the in-group, that is. Someone not in the know would not be able to understand an idiomatic usage by interpreting the meaning of the constituent words. So, in addition to making language more colorful, using idioms is a way to bind insiders and separate them from outsiders. Slang and professional jargon have similar functions. Their enduring popularity implies that we enjoy something about these prefabricated, presolved language puzzles.

On Englishes

I should slightly modify my earlier statement that I am monolingual. I'm fluent in three Englishes: English English, i.e., English as spoken in England and other parts of the United Kingdom; American English, as spoken in the United States and increasingly everywhere

---

* *In ancient Greece, every nine days 6,000 men were needed for a people's assembly. Those not attending were rounded up by authorities using a red-painted rope that left them "marked men."*[2]

else; and Indian English, as spoken in the nation that at the moment has the second largest number of English speakers in the world. Linguists consider each of these as having some degree of separate identity. Many of you will have heard the quotation attributed to Winston Churchill explaining the relationship of two of my Englishes—that the U.S. and the U.K. are "two nations divided by a common language." As regards Indian English, no speaker of another English would use a word like "prepone." You can probably easily unpack its morphemes to decipher that it means to reschedule something by bringing it earlier (rather than postponing it). As Nicholas Ostler points out in his monumental history of languages, *Empires of the Word,* English (of any kind) as a first language has peaked demographically.[3] The natives of lands where it is the first language, to borrow and abuse a term from nuclear physics, aren't sufficiently fast breeders. The future of the Englishes will likely be dominated by those who use them as a second language.

On Ludic* Language and the Seriousness of Humor
Our brains seem to be built to enjoy language novelty and word play. As David Crystal, the prominent language expert, notes in the very first sentence of his excellent

---

* *Not the language of the Ludians, though there is a language by that name, spoken by 3,000 people in the Baltic-Finnic family. This is a term derived from the Latin* ludus, *"play," and used by David Crystal to describe universal word play.*

book on the subject, called *Language Play:* "Everyone seems to engage in or respond to language play." He also points out that two-thirds of jokes in a typical collection depend on word play.

Speaking of humor, I recently heard some wonderful language to describe why it's such a serious business. Bob Mankoff, current editor of the *New Yorker* cartoons, said in a *Charlie Rose Show* interview that he thought of humor as a "counterweight to the hegemony of reason."[4] That sentiment is well supplemented by the following quotation from Clive James,[5] an encyclopedically accomplished commentator on culture: "The idea—an idea built into the English language over centuries of comic richness—is that learning and knowledge must be kept in balance. ..." As we'll see in the following chapters, there is much other scientific weight being added to counter this hegemony of reason. Since the Enlightenment, rationality and dispassionate logic have been given more than their due. Our minds are not as reason-able as we like to think.

On Scientific Correctness and Being "Sciencey"

Within the bounds of my natural laissez-fair* leanings, I have striven to be as correct as possible with the science in this book. Despite attempts to take occasional comedic license, I have stuck as closely as possible to the best reported relevant science I can find. I have tried to

---

* *Not the closely related term for governmental laxity (from French "allow to do"). Here I mean equanimity of laxity—to devote equally less effort to each relevant area.*

ensure that the contents of this book are "sciencey." I'm deeply indebted to the incomparable and incorrectable Stephen Colbert's insightful coinage of "truthiness" as a model. "Sciencey" is to science as "truthy" is to truth. While it may not be accurate to the nth level of minutiae, it captures the essence, the emotional truth, the truthiness of the scientific facts.

Another way to put this is that I have tried to be "scientifically correct," which I define in contradistinction to being "politically correct." I have not let the fashion for oxymoronic *political correctness* stand in the way of speaking scientific truth to power, or to power's friends, or to the people power definitely needs to not offend, or to constituencies that power might possibly need help from. Armed with the *scientifically correct,* we should be prepared to speak truth to anyone.

However, I have to *caveat** that noting all that is *scientifically correct* is to some degree subject to being overthrown by better evidence. Though you shouldn't let that technicality encourage you to hold out hope of the repeal of the fact of, say, gravity!

On Awareness of the Incorrectness of Some Scientific Language
I've tried wherever possible to prune away the complexities of scientific language. See if you can guess what the following *tongue-&-thought-twisting* language might mean. Firstly "mutually regulating

---

* *Intentionally used as a verb; see "Shakespeared Brain" point later (plus I'm tired of being a sticklee).*

psychobiological units"[6] and secondly "the cognitive-affective state characterized by intrusive and obsessive fantasizing concerning reciprocity of amorant feelings by the object of amorance." Extra points for those who guessed that the former means any emotionally close pair, e.g., friends or a couple. The latter, in 127 fewer letters, means love. Points deducted for anyone who knew already—since this implies complicity in these language crimes. Clearly, whatever other qualifications these folks have, scientists should not be left in charge of their own language. Less opaque scientists are trying to come up with much more easily understood terms. For example, in the area of the origin of language theories, folksy scientists have devised names like "bow-wow" theory, "poo-poo" theory, and "la-la" theory. We'll be looking at some of these in the following chapters.

On Clarifying Terms Used for Sciencey Lack of Awareness
States of lack of awareness are important throughout this book. Idioms in a sense require us to ignore our awareness of the meanings of their constituent words. Something we do without giving it a second (or first conscious) thought. Beyond just idioms, as Stephen Pinker, a leading psycholinguist and science writer, notes, "Most information processing in the brain is unconscious."[7] I have become aware that the terms used to describe such states of lack of awareness in scientific, and particularly in sciencey, literature are confusing. They carry so much

old baggage, so many unintended undercurrents, that additional clarity is required. Hence, to describe the state of the information processing that we are not aware of, rather than using the word "subconscious," which too often slips into Freudian territory, or "unconscious," which too often implies complete insensibility, I prefer to use the easier to keep distinct term "non-conscious." By *non-conscious* I mean fully awake but below the level of conscious awareness. Non-conscious does not necessarily mean irrational, nor does it necessarily mean only emotional. It seems we are built to have our conscious minds operate on a need-to-know basis. They are meant to be kept mostly *in the dark*. And they need only be interrupted when it's really essential or when it's already safe. They aren't so useful for anything that's fast, or dangerous.

On Listfulness Herein

I've only loosely organized these idioms into chapters, by theme. To these I've added a little light-minded commentary on mostly related topics with some tangential excursions. Thus the bulk of this book consists of lists of idioms. Rather than *lead you by the nose* through this maze of intentionally mis-understandable metaphors, I'd prefer to provide unmediated access to the lists, thereby leaving you the joy of discovering your own connections and resonances. It's a wonderful thought that you and the lists can make your own sweet, beautiful meaning together.

PREBUTTALS—ASSORTED APOLOGIES IN ADVANCE

To Aspiring Multilinguals

The source language forms of the selected idioms have not been included. This is for reasons of space and economy (of my effort). This book isn't intended to be a language reference. I'm assuming it's unlikely that many readers will go to places where the Russian words for "I'm not hanging noodles on your ears" would be useful. If you find yourself needing such words, I'm afraid you will need a more educationally oriented book.

To Aspired Multilinguals Who May Be Surprised or Offended

For speakers of any of these languages who have never heard of some of these idioms, or who might disagree with a translation, or who might be offended at a misrepresentation or a lost nuance—I apologize almost wholeheartedly. I can't vouch for every one of these idioms; some may no longer be in common active use. All I can say for sure is that each was considered, by the compilers of my sources, as being worthy of inclusion in their books. We are all at the mercy of various translators, upon whose good faith we must rely.

To Etymologists and Vocabularians

I haven't even tried to explain or trace the origins of these many idioms. That would have taken far too long. I was also dissuaded by the challenges intrinsic to lexical archaeology. Too much of the relevant detail is entombed forever in the substrata of our cultural history. Even that mighty word-watcher extraordinaire William Safire bows to the difficulties. As he says in his excellent collection of "On Language" columns published in book form as *The Right Word in the Right Place at the Right Time,* "The source of the expression 'to pull the wool over your eyes' is a mystery."[8] Though he finds a first usage (*Jamestown Journal,* 1839) and posits a theory, he concedes that "no etymologist has yet come up with the specific item made of wool." And I can be no match. As any good laissez-fairer would, I pre-capitulate.

However, if it turns out that enough people are interested, perhaps a wonderfully wikied* (and laissez-fairy) way of dealing with the enormity of this challenge might be the establishment of a new sport: WWWF (Worldwide Word Watching Federation) Competitive Etymology, in which volunteer vocabularians with sufficient stamina can engage in a WWWF Track-Down.

PREFACE, PREAMBLE, & PRELIMINARIES

*Here are five reasons to be curious** about languages:*
• First, languages provide a wonderful window into other peoples and how they see the world. You've

---

* *Not a misspelling of evil intent, but meant in the sense of Wikipedia: efforts of collective commoners.*
** *My favorite definition of curiosity comes from one of my least favorite philosophers—Thomas Hobbes; he whose nasty and brutish influence has not been sufficiently short. He called it a "lust of the mind."*

probably heard the not-so-*urban legend* about the Inuit having many words for snow. The validity of that claim is disputed by linguists, who say many of those snowy words are just modifications of a small number of root words.[9] You might, however, *raise an eyebrow* at the less well-known fact that Albanians, also presumably confronted with environmental excesses, have an excess of words for facial hair. These include "long broomlike moustache with bushy ends" and eyebrows that are "arched like the crescent moon." While we are on the subject: Italians have an expression for a "woman with a moustache who is attractive" and Arabs have a contrariwise proverb that pleads "may God protect us from hairy women and beardless men." The Danish recognize the limitations of facial hair in their proverb "if a beard were all, the goat would be the winner." Whilst I'm in no position to adjudicate the worthiness of urban language legends, it does make intuitive sense that languages are exquisitely attuned to the environments and predilections of their speakers. For example, the Marovo speakers of the Solomon Islands have a single word to describe "the behavior of groups of fish when individuals drift, circle, and float as if drunk." There's nothing *fishy* (or, as a similarly suspicious German might say, nothing "totally pure rabbit" or the Chinese "under a plum tree") about these people's being keenly interested in which *side their bread is buttered on.*

• Second, language provides a wonderful window into other people, i.e., other specific individuals. A sentiment wonderfully and briefly encapsulated in a quotation from Ben Jonson, one of Shakespeare's rivals: "Language most shows a man. Speak that I might see thee."

• Third, language provides a wonderful window that also works the other way. Looking in that direction provides entrée into another exotic and intriguing world, the insides of our own heads. For example, analyzing the associations implicit in our understanding of words can show how quickly we judge people by their appearances. Careful measurements, down to the millisecond level, show that we are hard-wired to notice race and gender. The average person registers the race of another human face in less than a hundred milliseconds, and gender in another 50 milliseconds.[10] There will be more details on this, and much else in language that can be used to *shed light on* our insides, in the following chapters.

• Fourth, we should all pay close attention to language because it can have such powerful conscious effects. Benjamin Disraeli, twice the British Prime Minister in the 19th century, is famous for having said, "with words we govern men." I'm not so well read that I knew that. I'm indebted to William Safire, the American English–speaking world's most prominent self-confessed word maven. He uses it as inspiration for his own extension "by proverbs we enliven copy."[11] Which I can stretch further to say "by idioms we enliven speech." The original quotation describes the conscious use of language as an instrument of power in the public arena. Something Americans in particular understand and respect. Their constitution is considered their founding sacred text.

• Fifth, the power and influence of language also operates at much more personal levels and in much less explicit ways. To quote George Lakoff, the prominent cognitive linguist: "Language usually works through the cognitive unconscious, so we are mostly unaware of the effects it's having."[12] We'll return to more of his views later, when we summarize his call for a New Enlightenment to address the increasingly apparent shortcomings of the First. An experiment conducted at New York University shows how language exposure, even if inadvertent, can have very measurable effects on behaviour. Researchers asked students to volunteer for an experiment in which they completed a word-based task (constructing grammatically correct sentences from lists of words). However, unbeknownst to the students, the experiment hadn't ended when they left. The time it took them to walk down the exit corridor was measured surreptitiously. Students whose lists had contained words associated with old age (like retired or wrinkled) walked more slowly, by 13 percent, than those whose word lists were neutral. The words they had been exposed to measurably changed the speed at which they walked.[13] That's staggering. And alarming.

OK, enough preamble. Please join me on a trip of the tongues, through the world's idioms ... and along the way, into the inside of heads ... of others and of our own selves.

Dry firewood meets a flame
Chinese: instant attraction

chapter one

THE LANGUAGE OF LOVE

Swallowed like a postman's sock

Languages make visible what's important to their users. And what could be more important than love? Some paleolinguists have proposed that language developed for romantic purposes. Though, to be more precise, they mean for mating, not dating. Dating is an evolutionarily recent phenomenon that we aren't well adapted to. Speaking of evolution, Darwin proposed an early version of this theory. In *The Descent of Man* he wrote, "Some early progenitor of man probably first used his voice in producing true musical cadences, that is in singing … and … this power would have been especially exerted during the courtship of the sexes."[1] Music may have been the audition, as well as the *food of love*. This view of language-origin-ology is known as "la-la" theory.

La-la theory has languished unloved since Darwin's time. Its *old flame* has only recently been rekindled (as the Italians would say, like "reheated cabbage"), for example in Geoffrey Miller's Mating Mind

Theory.[2] The modern version has expanded far beyond the analogy with the songs of courting animals to include many aspects of complex evolutionary psychology. So perhaps "la-la" as a folksy name is no longer satisfying. I propose "woo-woo" theory as a better nickname to encompass its increased scope. Ardent woo-woo theorists believe language (and other sophisticated mental and behavioral traits) gained considerable complexity in the competition to impress the opposite sex. Their theory leads them to the deliciously seductive point of view that the human brain fits the profile of a "sexually selected ornament."

The peacock tail* is one of nature's most flagrant sexually selected ornaments. It clearly doesn't fit the *survival of the fittest* model, in which animals are ruthlessly honed to be lean, mean, survival machines. Instead, peacock tails became ostentatious, so much bigger and unfit compared to peahen tails (which are a drab gray), in hot pursuit of the *survival of the sexiest scenario*—i.e., animals are not so lean, not so mean, courtship machines. Often what makes you fittest makes you sexiest, but not always. The peacock tail is a substantial survival liability. And surviving in spite of it is precisely what the peacock is advertising. Many sex selection characteristics in nature are driven by the needs of males to attract the attention of choosy females. Usually it's that way around; Mother Nature

---

* *The peacock's tail is featured in the very unsexy Polish idiom "to show the peacock," which means to vomit.*

mandates that it's usually females who get to pick their mates. And I can confirm from my own fieldwork that human females fit this model. They are certainly very choosy (i.e., woo-woe theory). However, to be considered a *catch*, it's not enough to just catch a female's eye; males, to pass along their genes, also have to pass the females' further selection tests (perhaps the origin of the idiomatic expression *to make a pass*?). And that's where conspicuous excess in language and other higher brain functions comes in. We ornament ourselves with language to advertise our impressive brains, and our access to expensive resources like education and leisure time. Mother Nature has forced men to become *blinguists*.

Speaking of Mother Nature—she is an example of one of the few remaining aspects of English that are assigned a grammatical gender. English is unusually sexless. Many other languages have much more gender specificity. Most other European languages are more sexful—having male, female, and neuter. Though languages don't have to stop at just three genders. Bantu languages can have more than ten. Confused? Grammatical genders are more clearly referred to as noun classes, which can impose certain rules on the way other words are modified.

Gender distinctions may not be as spurious as the *politically correct* might like to think. With all due disrespect, *political correctness* is, in my view, a particularly nonsensical expression, which makes it inadvertently idiomatic. Political views and power interests vary considerably, and we could all benefit from encouraging diversity of opinions in our politics. Efforts to avoid giving offense to any constituency can cause worse offenses against reason. Which is how this ill-formed expression can become a dangerous idea.

Given prevailing *politically correct*-ed sentiments, you might be surprised to learn that the *scientifically correct* data show that women's brains are smaller than men's, by around 10 percent when adjusted for relative body size differences.[3] Scientists don't really know, and perhaps are afraid to try to find out, why. However, before the *male chauvinist pigs* out there start *making hay* with that, Neanderthal brains were larger than ours. And in relation to language, bragging rights go the other way. The relevant areas of women's brains are denser—by 12 percent—and better connected than men's. Women's brains also contain more gray matter, whereas men's have more white matter. Gender differences appear very early. Developmental psychologists have shown that babies less than two days young have clearly different preferences for what they stare at. Baby girls prefer to stare at faces, whereas baby boys prefer to stare at mechanical objects.[4] Two days is too early for this to be entirely cultural.

Scientists of either gender, whatever their innate preferences and however they were socialized, don't yet know whether to *make head or tails* of all that. However, to connect the earlier point on tails with these points on heads, woo-woo theorists argue that these comparatively small differences between human male and female brains are an indication that, for us, sexual selection goes both ways. Men can also be choosy. And that has led to human females being more conspicuously ornamented than other species.

The way other languages look at love can also shed light on distinctions that aren't so easily made in English. Ancient Greek had four distinct words for different kinds of love: affectionate, as between family members; companionate, a dispassionate virtuous love, as between friends or those with common interests; charitable, as toward those who are not family or friends; and erotic, which was passionate and romantic and which could also but need not necessarily be sexual. English love is comparatively confusing. As the French say, it leaves you "not knowing which foot to dance on" or, as the Spanish say, it makes you feel like "mambo in the head."

Though theories of language origin-ology are still in hot dispute, whatever the experts finally conclude, it's certainly true that love and language are passionately intertwined. So let's take a look at how idioms feature in that torrid entanglement:

When English speakers are madly in love—we say we are *head over heels,* which is oddly the way we usually are, i.e., upright. Earlier versions of this idiom were to be "heels over head," but that's now been turned on its head.

Similarly blessed, Germans get a little more anatomically specific; they are "neck over head," or they say they are "in love until over both ears." The equivalent in Colombian Spanish is the considerably less appealing "swallowed like a postman's sock." As English speakers, when we might *sow wild oats,* the French, to show off their supposed greater prowess, "strike the 400 blows." The French have an expression that, literally translated, means "by candlelight a goat looks like a lady." Don't be too alarmed that it's the equivalent of the Italian admonition not to choose "a jewel, or a woman, or linen, by candlelight." But don't put your worries about French romance and goats to bed just yet; they also have an expression that literally translated is "a lover of a goat whose hair is combed," which means a man who is attracted to any woman, or a womanizer. To further emphasize the need for caution in regard to French romance, even when there are no goats involved, they have sayings that translate as "love is blind, which is why it's usually preceded by touch" and the equally unromantic "love is blind but marriage restores sight." The Spanish have an expression indicating that their goats are on the other end of such matters; in Spanish, "a kid goat" means a womanizer. In Italian a "male goat" means someone who has been cheated on. But getting back to the French, and by way of explanation for the success of Gérard Depardieu's film career, the French have a proverb indicating that "a big nose never spoiled a handsome face."

Turning to Italians, also supposedly great lovers, while we might *rekindle an old flame,* they, less flatteringly, "reheat cabbage." Italians also have a proverb that warns against the potential dangers of too much cabbage reheating, which says, "leave women alone and go study mathematics." It's not so clear how successful that advice has been, given that there aren't so many world-famous Italian mathematicians. Italians also bring goats into their romantic proverbs: "a goose, a woman, and a goat, are bad things lean."

Lover of a goat whose hair is combed
French: a man attracted to any woman

An English husband might be *under his wife's thumb,* whereas a similarly oppressed Japanese would be "under his wife's buttocks." It's not just individuals who can fall under the spell of a beautiful woman; the Chinese compliment "lovely enough to cause the fall of a city" attests to their equivalent of Helen of Troy. Perhaps the oddest romance-related idiom, however, is the Spanish "to pluck the turkey." There is no English equivalent; it's usually translated as "to make love at a window"! I'm guessing that you might have a similar reaction to mine in that you wonder if this is such a popular Spanish pastime that they would need an idiom for it? However, it's not as alarmingly exhibitionist as it sounds. What they mean is that older sense of "to make love," i.e., to flirt or court, and it relates to the practice of a gentlemen sweet talking (or, as the Japanese might say, "talking through the nose") to a lady who was at her window balcony above (à la Romeo and Juliet).

ROMANCE STARTS WITH A SUITABLE FIRST IMPRESSION

- To get one's eyes stolen: *to be dazzled (Japanese)*
- To throw face: *to make a good impression (Spanish, El Salvador)*
- To be struck by lightning*: *instant attraction (Italian)*
- To be struck by a thunderbolt: *instant attraction (French)*
- Dry firewood meets a flame: *instant attraction (Chinese)*

---

* This is the original meaning of the word "astonishment."

FOLLOWED BY COMPLIMENTS AND SWEET TALK

- To speak through the nose: *sweet talk (Japanese)*
- A bonbon and me with diabetes: *a street compliment (Spanish, Latin America)*
- What curves and me without brakes: *a street compliment (Spanish, Latin America)*
- Fritter: *an attractive man (Spanish, Peru)*
- Little mango: *hot, sexy (Spanish, Latin America)*
- Biscuit: *hot, sexy, attractive (Spanish, Mexico)*
- To be a monkey face: *cute (Spanish, Mexico)*

Thighs shaped like banana trees
Bengali: compliment to an attractive woman

- Very drinkable: *attractive (Spanish, Mexico)*
- Thighs shaped like banana trees: *a compliment to an attractive woman (Bengali)*
- To set the dogs on someone: *to flirt (Spanish, Latin America)*
- Lovely enough to cause the fall of a city: *stunning (Chinese)*
- Hen's egg: *darling (French)*
- Piece of the moon: *a lovely or handsome person (Hindi)*
- Lotus-eyed: *beautiful eyes (Hindi)*
- Having the waist of an elegant lion: *an attractive woman (Hindi)*
- A butterfly: *a showily dressed or flirtatious woman (Hindi)*
- All sixteen (traditional) adornments: *an elaborately made-up woman (Hindi)*
- Like hibiscus rising out of water: *grace of a woman (Chinese)*

WHICH MIGHT LEAD TO A DATE. BUT THE OBJECT OF YOUR AFFECTIONS MIGHT NOT SHOW UP

- To give the package: *to stand someone up (Italian)*
- To lay a rabbit: *to stand someone up (French)*
- To take a jacket: *to stand someone up (French)*
- To wind up like a traffic light: *to be stood up, left hanging (Spanish, Nicaragua)*

OR IF HE DOES, HE MIGHT NOT TURN OUT TO BE IDEAL

- Heart thief: *heart breaker (Italian)*
- To give squash or pumpkins: *to stand someone up (Spanish, Latin America)*
- Autumn sky: *to be fickle (Japanese)*
- The space below a nose is long: *to be lewd toward women (Japanese)*
- A trick of color: *a pretense of love (Japanese)*
- To have fast hands: *to be a womanizer (Japanese)*
- To drain one's horns: *to sow one's wild oats (German)*

To give squash / pumpkins
Spanish (Latin America): to stand someone up

- To strike the 400 blows: *to sow one's wild oats (French)*
- A pigeon fancier: *a lady's man (Hindi)*
- Bitten by the spider: *fickle or flirtatious (Spanish, Chile)*
- Having seven husbands: *loose woman (Hindi)*
- A wild gourd: *a beautiful but worthless person (Hindi)*
- Unable to stop being the owl: *can't stop flirting (Italian)*
- To burn grilled rice cakes: *to be jealous (Japanese)*
- Hole filler: *someone to date between relationships (German)*
- An apron hunter: *a womanizer (German)*
- A kid goat: *a womanizer or man who lives off women (Spanish, Central America)*

HOWEVER, IF IT DOES GO WELL ... YOU MIGHT

- Flannel: *make out (Spanish, Uruguay & Argentina)*
- Drinking the lip: *kiss (Hindi)*
- Tooth-gift: *a love bite (Hindi)*
- Ham: *French kiss (Spanish, Venezuela)*
- Have one's atoms hooked together: *really hit it off (French)*
- Buckle polish: *slow dance (Spanish, Venezuela)*
- Shake the skeleton: *dance (Spanish, Latin America)*
- Wiggle your bucket: *dance (Spanish, Mexico)*
- Throw a foot: *shake a leg, dance (Spanish, Cuba)*
- Get the moths off: *dance (Spanish, Mexico)*
- Pluck the turkey: *make love at a window (Spanish)*

WHICH MIGHT LEAD TO BECOMING YOUR BELOVED'S ...

- Half orange: *sweetheart, spouse, soul mate* (*Spanish, Latin America*)
- To be sweet potato with: *to be madly in love with* (*Spanish, Costa Rica*)
- To be in love until over both ears: *to be madly in love* (*German*)
- To be someone's leg: *to be a main squeeze* (*Spanish, Chile*)
- Goat: *partner, boyfriend, girlfriend* (*Spanish, Costa Rica*)
- Bumblebee: *sweetheart* (*Spanish, Chile*)

AND THINGS MIGHT GET SERIOUS

- Swallowed like a postman's sock: *hopelessly in love* (*Spanish, Colombia*)
- Like water for chocolate: *the boiling point of one's passion (or anger)* (*Spanish*)
- To fall neck over head in love: *to be madly in love, head over heels in love* (*German*)
- To scorch one's own body: *to be consumed with love* (*Japanese*)
- Love without memory: *to be madly in love* (*Russian*)
- To have eaten a monkey: *to be nuts about* (*German*)
- To be asphyxiated: *to be in love* (*Spanish, Dominican Republic*)

AND IT COULD GET VERY SERIOUS

*Apologies in advance if much of the following seems negative
and sexist. Please don't shoot the messenger; I'm constrained
by my source material.*

- To solidify one's body: *to get married (Japanese)*
- Blooming flowers and a full moon: *ideal time for
  a wedding (Chinese)*
- As happy as a fiancée: *happy as a lark, the highest
  happiness (Russian)*
- To distribute cardamoms: *to invite to a marriage (Hindi)*
- Matricide: *marriage (Spanish, Costa Rica)*
- To hang oneself: *to get married (Spanish, Mexico)*
- To stain [a girl's] hands with turmeric: *to marry
  (Hindi)*
- Handcuffs: *the wife (Spanish, Latin America)*
- War Department: *ironic term for wife (Spanish, Mexico)*
- The Holy Inquisition: *an inquisitive wife (Spanish,
  Mexico)*
- To be under a bonnet: *to be married (German)*
- She who sits at [one's] side: *a wife (Hindi)*
- Life-lord, the support of life: *husband (Hindi)*
- Has him in her fist: *has him under her thumb, under
  her control (Spanish)*
- The seven utterances: *the marriage vows (Hindi)*
- To be under the wife's buttocks: *to be henpecked
  (Japanese)*

To hang oneself
Spanish (Mexico): to get married

- To stand under the slipper*: *to be henpecked (German)*
- To be under his wife's shoe: *to be henpecked (Russian)*
- The cricket on the stove: *a submissive wife (German)*
- The wind from a woman's shawl strikes: *under female influence (Hindi)*
- Oversized pants: *a man pushed around by his wife or girlfriend (Spanish)*
- Love is blind, but marriage restores your sight: *unromantic proverb (French)*

---

* Those romantic Germans have a word that translates as "dragon fodder," for the gift a husband gives to apologize to his wife.

HOWEVER, IT MIGHT NOT ALL BE ROSY. THERE MIGHT BE SOME PROBLEMS

- An autumn breeze begins to blow: *a mutual cooling of love (Japanese)*
- The tomatoes have faded: *the love is gone (Russian)*
- To do the horns to someone: *to be unfaithful (Italian, Russian)*
- To have horns: *to have been cheated on (Italian)*
- Decorated one: *someone whose wife has been unfaithful (Spanish, Chile)*
- A red apricot goes over the wall: *a married woman takes a lover (Chinese)*
- To take a rake: *to be dumped (French)*
- To be laid flat: *to be dumped (French)*
- To hit someone in the back of the neck: *to have an affair with someone's partner (Spanish, Chile)*
- To leave someone nailed: *to dump someone (Spanish)*
- Wearing a green hat: *having an unfaithful wife (Chinese)*
- You have a pretty green hat: *your wife is cheating on you (Chinese)*
- In buying horses and taking a wife, shut your eyes and pray to God: *proverb (Italian)*
- Eggs and vows are easily broken: *proverb (Japanese)*
- Never rely on love or the weather: *proverb (German)*
- To split a sleeve: *to break it off with someone (Japanese)*
- A male goat: *someone who has been cheated on (Italian)*

OTHER ROMANCE-RELATED IDIOMS

- There are no ugly 15-year-olds: *proverb (Spanish)*
- To live like an old farm rifle: *to be always pregnant (Spanish, Nicaragua)*
- Like hedgehogs: *very frisky (Italian)*
- To throw a gray hair: *to have a fling (Italian)*
- Reheated cabbage: *an attempt to revive a lapsed love affair (Italian)*
- Separation agent: *someone who breaks up a relationship for you (German)*
- Aunt seducer: *a young man whose manners are too good (German)*
- Leftover Christmas cake: *an unmarried woman over 25 (Japanese)*
- Green widow: *dirty or lewd old woman (Spanish, Mexico)*
- Woman with a green tail: *dirty or lewd old woman (Spanish, Mexico)*
- A yawning mussel: *to be amorous, horny (French)*
- An old schoolboy: *bachelor (Yiddish)*
- The bodiless one: *way of referring to Kamdev the god of love (Hindi)*
- By candlelight a goat looks like a lady: *proverb (French)*
- To stay behind to dress [statues of] saints: *to be an old maid (Spanish)*
- Shrimp: *man with nice body but ugly head (Spanish)*

An old schoolboy
Yiddish: a bachelor

chapter two

KITH & KIN-DRED

Seventh water on a starchy jelly

A s THE *politically corrected* proverbial idiom goes: No (hu)man is an island. That seems to be biologically true. We are evolved to live enmeshed in a network of social relationships, including as emotionally leaky and contagious "mutually regulating psychobiological units." Our identities are defined by our relationships, and language plays a role in all our identities.

At the closer and earlier *end of* our relationship *spectrum*—babies can distinguish at a very early age the sounds that are unique to their *mother tongues* (or should that be their mother's tongue?*). They develop a sense of the sound structure of their native language surprisingly early. Infant-ologists have demonstrated this by measuring the electrical activity of the brains of French and German babies. Each language puts different emphasis on the syllables of two-syllable words. German puts it on the first, French on the second. Infants showed a processing advantage for the rhythmic structure typical

---

* *Yiddish used to be known as "the mother's tongue" and was used mainly by women; men used Hebrew.*[1]

in their native language. The researchers concluded that language-specific neural representations of word forms are present in the infant brain as early as four months of age.[2]

Many families develop their own "familese." Children in particular have a strong inclination to fill holes in their language. As Barbara Wallraff notes in the introduction to her excellently amusing book on language holes, *Word Fugitives,*[3] we all have this urge. As she puts it, "The impulse to coin words today may well be a vestige of the impulse that gave mankind language in the first place." She also points out that around 40 percent of twins develop varying degrees of a private language. Paul Dickson has collected such familese in his great little book called *Family Words.* My favorites are: *condo-mini-home* for a small apartment; *menuitis** for having too many choices; and *nagrivation,* for arguments caused by attempts to get unlost. From my own family: When we were kids, my siblings would say "yemember?" as a contraction for "do you remember?"

Roy Blunt, Jr., that most astutely and acutely attuned word fancier, in his gemful** book *Alphabet Juice,* has an entry on familese. In it he discloses how the pronunciation of the name of the recent leader of Russia sounded to him like a typical familese word for an intimate body part.[4]

Finally, on the subject of kin, a wonderfully unkind, intentional mis-parsing, and repurpos-

---

* *Psychologists have measured this phenomenon.*
** *Gemful—a word Blount would no doubt think should be a word since* bejeweled *is too unwieldy.*

ing (hyphenated here for clarity), is *kin-dred:* "fear of family gatherings."[5]

Beyond our closest unchosen ties, couples often develop private new words, an idiolect, that are often childlike or childish.* The most embarrassing and alarming example I've ever come across is from one of America's most beloved presidents, Ronald Reagan. I must warn you that the following might permanently change your view of him. In a preemptive Valentine's Day note to his wife (on White House letterhead), dated February 4, he addresses her as "Mommie, Poo Pants, 1st Lady, Nancy" and signs himself as "Pappa, Poo Pants, 1st Guy, Ronnie."[6] I know … I know … That's shocking, revolting, and enough to make you want to curse. An unexpected collision of poo-poo and woo-woo theories.

Groups of friends, gangs, and whole communities develop slang as a way to establish and reinforce the in-group vs. out-group distinction. Professional communities do the same; they develop exclusive technical lingo to enshroud their specialized knowledge, which is why to a doctor a "heart attack" is a "myocardial infarction."

Another way that we use language to make finer-grained social distinctions is by gossiping. Evolutionary psychologists have proposed that the need for greater social coordination, bonding, and reputation management were all critical to language origin-ology. Our near-relative apes can tell us a thing or two about this. They use social grooming, actual nit-picking (painstaking combing through each

---

* Amorese *or* couplese, *though, often is just oh-plea-ese?*

other's fur), in the same way that we use language to gossip. Perhaps that might help explain why language teachers are so nit-picky about the rules of language? Continuing our effort to improve "sciencey" language, perhaps we could call this the "tut-tut" theory. Negative gossip is nine times more likely than positive gossip to be repeated and spread.[7]

Taking gossip to a national level, it's said that Italians are mama's boys, explaining why their related insult is "papa's boy." Italians call a high-ranking boss "mister sainted mother," combining the veneration of both mothers and religion. Children can be the *apple of our eye*; in China they are the "pearl in the palm." The Japanese extend similar imagery to extremes: "Even if one puts a child in one's eye, it doesn't hurt."

Where we can have friends who are like *two peas in a pod*, the Mexicans are much less appealingly like "fingernail and dirt." A similar Hindi-speaking pair could be described as the puzzlingly self-defeating "union of fire and water." Whereas for a Japanese to "smell of water" means to be distant and unfriendly.

MOTHER

- Mister sainted mother: *the big boss* (*Italian*)
- Co-mother of one's child: *close female friend* (*Spanish, Puerto Rico*)
- To throw mothers: *to curse, swear at* (*Spanish, Mexico*)

- The mother of the lamb: *the real reason for something* (*Spanish*)
- To dis-mother: *to beat up* (*Spanish, Mexico*)
- God cannot be everywhere, so he created mothers*: *proverb* (*Hebrew*)

FATHER

- Oh, you fat father: *good heavens* (*German*)
- A father is a banker provided by nature: *proverb* (*French*)
- Father of two tongues: *hypocritical, two-faced* (*Arabic*)
- Father of moustaches: *friendly, slightly mocking way of describing* (*Arabic*)
- A devil [curse] should enter your father's father: *insult* (*Yiddish*)
- Without father, mother, or dog that barks for me: *alone* (*Spanish*)
- Neither father or a son-in-law, nor a brother: *no relation* (*Russian*)

HUSBANDS & WIVES

- Life lord: *husband* (*Hindi*)
- Sister-in-law's brother: *husband* (*auspicious form*) (*Hindi*)
- She who sits at [one's] side: *wife* (*Hindi*)

---

* *To have a domineering mother—to live under a hegemomy.*

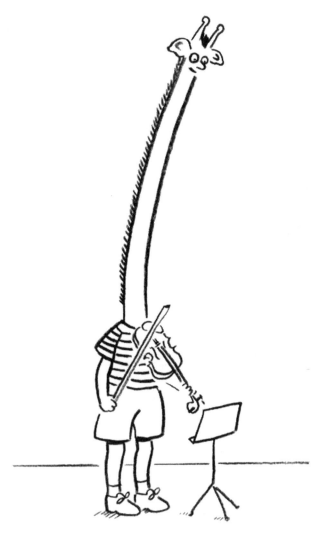

Giraffe child
Japanese: a prodigy

- Who sits at [her] husband's left: *wife (Hindi)*
- The Holy Inquisition: *your [inquiring] wife (Spanish, Mexico)*
- The cricket on the stove: *a submissive little wife, homebody (German)*
- Handcuffs: *the wife (Spanish, Latin America)*
- War Department: *ironic term for wife (Spanish, Mexico)*
- The rabbi's wife: *a pompous woman (Yiddish)*

CHILDREN

- Fruit of heaven: *offspring (Hindi)*
- Crystallization of love: *child (Japanese)*
- A giraffe child: *a prodigy (Japanese)*
- A grain of seed: *an only child (Japanese)*
- To eat like a child of God (an orphan): *to eat fast (Spanish, Mexico)*
- Even if one puts a child in one's eye, it doesn't hurt: *apple of one's eye (Japanese)*
- A daughter of yesterday: *unexpected, not altogether welcome (Arabic)*
- A pearl in the palm: *a beloved daughter (Chinese)*
- A pearl from an old oyster: *the birth of a son in later years (Chinese)*
- The son of a duck is a floater: *like father like son (Arabic)*
- Children of well-fed families: *good-for-nothing sons of the idle rich (Chinese)*

- An eye of tea: *playful, mischievous child (Japanese)*
- The light of a dark house: *an only son, a beautiful child or person (Hindi)*
- It is easier to rule a nation than a son: *proverb (China)*
- The light of a dark house: *an only son (Hindi)*

GRANDKIN

- There's Grandma for you: *a fine kettle of fish (Russian)*
- Tell this to your grandmother: *I was not born yesterday (Russian)*
- My grandmother's taste: *bad taste (Yiddish)*
- Grandma's summer: *Indian summer (Russian)*
- Grandmother story: *fairy tale, unbelievable story (Yiddish)*
- Grandmother was ambiguous: *it remains to be seen (Russian)*
- Because his grandmother smokes: *for no good reason (Spanish)*
- Don't push Grandma into the nettles; she's not wearing her knickers: *proverb (French)*
- A house with an old grandparent harbors a jewel: *proverb (China)*
- Eat sweets and play with grandchildren: *a carefree life in old age (Chinese)*
- A piece of pleasure: *grandchild (Yiddish)*

OTHER KIN

- Burn beanstalks to cook beans: *fight among brothers (Chinese)*
- Of the same milk: *a sister (Hindi)*
- By a different belly: *half-siblings with different mothers (Japanese)*
- Seventh (or tenth) water on a starchy jelly: *a kissing cousin (Russian)*
- What the mother-in-law sees: *superficially clean part of the house (Spanish)*
- To treat like a stepmother: *to treat shabbily (German)*
- A stepmother's face: *an unsmiling face (Chinese)*

An onion shared with a friend tastes like roast lamb
Arabic (Egypt): proverb

- Revenge for the daughter-in-law: *even the score* (*Russian*)
- Bare branches: *a man without a bride, due to one child policy* (*Chinese*)
- An un-housed spirit: *a man who dies childless* (*Hindi*)
- An old schoolboy: *a bachelor* (*Yiddish*)

To fix the cake
Spanish: to patch things up

FRIENDS

- To be made syrup: *to be friendly and affable (Spanish)*
- Be on a short leg: *on friendly terms (Russian)*
- My crazy one: *my friend (Spanish, Dominican Republic)*
- Honeycomb: *long-term group of friends (Spanish, Dominican Republic)*
- To be fingernail and flesh: *to be very close (Spanish)*
- To eat out of the same plate: *to be on friendly terms (Spanish, Mexico)*
- To be fingernail and dirt: *on friendly terms (Spanish, Mexico)*
- Carry on bread and salt: *to be good friends (Russian)*
- The union of fire and water: *close friendship (Hindi)*
- To exchange turbans: *close friends (Hindi)*
- Two halves of a gram seed: *blood brothers (Hindi)*
- To compare each other's liver and gall: *close friends (Japanese)*
- To get along like buttocks and shirt: *great friends (French)*
- The skin matches: *to get along well (Japanese)*
- A hair of the moustache: *an intimate friend (Hindi)*
- An onion shared with a friend tastes like roast lamb: *proverb (Arabic, Egypt)*
- To come for fire: *to pay a brief visit (Hindi)*
- Visit rarely, and you will be more loved: *proverb (Arabic)*
- He who lends to a friend loses twice: *proverb (French)*
- Guests always give pleasure—when they arrive or when they leave: *proverb (Portuguese)*

A dog and a monkey
Japanese: to be on bad terms

NOT SUCH GOOD FRIENDS

- To smell like water: *unfriendly, formal situation (Japanese)*
- Migratory crow: *a fair-weather friend (Hindi)*
- Those who seek a constant friend go to the cemetery: *proverb (Russia)*
- Meal finished, friendship ended: *someone who eats and runs (Spanish)*
- Meeting the Buddha in hell: *a friend in need is a friend indeed (Japanese)*
- Monkey's friendship: *fickle friendship (Hindi)*

- A quarrel in a neighbor's house is refreshing: *proverb (India)*
- A guest and a fish after three days are poison: *proverb (French)*
- A dog and a monkey: *to be on bad terms (Japanese)*
- Porch dog: *a hanger-on, parasite (Hindi)*
- A honeyed knife: *a secret enemy (Hindi)*
- A sleeve: *an enemy in the guise of a friend (Hindi)*
- Cannot share the same sky: *irreconcilable, deep hatred for (Chinese)*
- To fix the cake: *to patch things up (Spanish)*

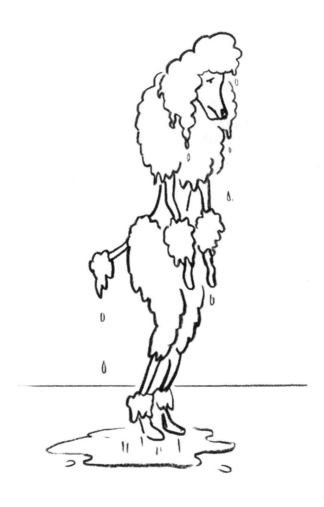

To stand like a watered poodle
German: to be crestfallen

chapter three

ANIMALS

Here the donkey falls

L ANGUAGE WAS THOUGHT to be uniquely human. Something that distinguished us from other animals. I like that way of putting it. Since we too often forget that we, too, are animals. As Christine Kenneally reports in her wonderful book on the development of language, *The First Word,* amazing animals are helping us redefine how we think, not only of them, but also of language itself.[1] Scientists used to think of language as a monolithic capability; however, animals are showing us that it is more accurately thought of as a suite of capabilities. And it turns out that many of those abilities are shared with other animals.

At the low end of animal communications, Kenneally notes that vervet monkeys have a preprogrammed three-alarm call vocabulary. The equivalent of "Yikes! There's an X!", where "X" could be a leopard, an eagle, or a snake. Further up the communication chain is Kanzi,* an alpha male bonobo (pygmy chimpanzee). He understands a

---

* *Kanzi's story is serendipitous. Researchers were trying to teach his mother; he was just along for the ride. She wasn't a good student, but Kanzi inadvertently got the hang of it.*

couple of thousand words and can communicate using 300 gestures, a custom keyboard (we're not talking QWERTY here), and pictogram sheets.

Remarkably, Kanzi is a word coiner. He was able to creatively fill a gap in his vocabulary. He spontaneously combined "water" and "bird" to form "waterbird" to refer to a duck. Kanzi has shown that bonobos can acquire language skills equivalent to a human infant (about two and half years old). And even more so than for other infants, the expression "cheeky monkey" seems most apt. One of the new sentences Kanzi correctly understood was, "Can I tickle your butt?" That might not be so surprising for those familiar with other famous bonobo characteristics. A final point on the *monkey business* of ape linguistics is related to my favorite guinea pig name. In a wonderful piece of punery, researchers at Columbia University called one of their simian subjects Nim* Chimpsky, in humorous homage to Noam Chomsky, the founder of modern linguistics.

Language capabilities aren't confined to species that we consider our near relatives. Some researchers believe that the prize for the animal with the most advanced grasp of human syntax and semantics should have gone to Alex, an African gray parrot in the lab of Irene Pepperberg at Brandeis University. He was no *bird brain* and could identify 50 objects and use conceptual categories for color, shape, and number.** All

---

* *A half-syllable away from the slightly more apt Nym (since that's a morpheme indicating naming).*

** *Sadly Alex, to put it Python-esquely, is an ex-parrot. His last words to Pepperberg were reported to have been "I love you."*[2]

of these had been thought to be uniquely human abilities. Ironically, linguists call the type of language that Pepperberg used to talk to Alex a "pidgin." Alex was estimated to have the language skills of a two-year-old human and the cognitive abilities of a six-year-old.[3]

As Jonah Lehrer reports in his intriguing book *Proust Was a Neuroscientist*, bird brains have also proved crucial in groundbreaking brain science. Neuro-anatomists first directly observed the once-thought impossible, the formation of new brain cells in bird brains. In a wonderful connection with Charles Darwin's la-la theory, it seems that to sing their complex melodies, male birds need to make new brain cells every day.[4] And this need is influenced by environmental factors. Birds stuck in sterile lab environments have no need to and don't make new brain cells. This work has been replicated in primate brains and, by extension, applies to us. A whole new field of neurogenesis is emerging, and among its initial areas of interest is a new class of antidepressant drugs aimed at improving neurogenesis. It seems that new brain cells, some of which come from new experiences and needing to learn new things, can make us happier! We are neophiles built to be happier when we are stimulated.

To summarize the state of the art of "woo-woo theory," I can put it no better than George Miller, its founder: "Creative courtship may have also played upon neophilia, a fundamental attentional and cognitive attraction to novelty.... Darwin argued that neophilia was an important factor in the diversification and rapid evolution of bird song. Primate and human neophilia is especially strong.... Partners who offered more cognitive variety and creativity in their relationships may have had longer, more reproductively successful relationships.... A good sense of humor is the most sexually attractive variety of creativity, and human mental evolution is better imagined as a romantic comedy than as a story of disaster, warfare, predation, and survival."*[5] He doesn't go into the fact that many of today's romantic comedies involve their share of disaster and gender warfare....

Any tale of animal linguistics wouldn't be complete without *a shaggy dog story*. "Rico," a border collie at the Max Planck Institute in Germany, could interpret the meanings of hundreds of words and could even infer the meanings of new ones. When commanded to enter a room and retrieve an object he had never seen before, he was correctly able to pick the one object he hadn't previously learned the word for. And let's not forget "Lassie," who had a particularly useful command of disaster-**related vocabulary. Daniel Dennett, the famous cognitive scientist, describes words as being "like sheepdogs herding ideas."

It appears that other species share another important aspect of human communications. Kenneally reports on what happened when one ape trained in sign language

---

* *Woo-woo theory now seems less apt; we need to emphasize the creative and humorous aspects of relationships. Perhaps "new ha woo" might be better?*

** *Disaster originally meant "under a bad star."*

first met another equally proficient ape. They had a sign-shouting match. Neither ape was willing to listen. The French have a great expression for it, "the dialogue of the deaf."

At least at the moment, it's still not controversial that humans are the only species using complex symbols. And no non-human animal has ever been observed using an idiom. That, at least, is still uniquely human.

Even though animals don't use idioms, they are very widely used in them:

When we *smell a rat* or feel that *something is fishy,* a similarly suspicious Frenchman would be concerned that "there's an eel under the rock," a cautious German would worry that something wasn't "totally pure rabbit," and an Italian would say, "Here the cat broods." Our cats have more time to brood, since they have nine lives; Italian canines are similarly, though slightly less blessed, as they have "seven lives like a dog." While it can *rain cats and dogs* here, German weather is less inclusive—it only "rains young dogs."

We have difficulty with careless penmanship seen as *chicken scratch.* For the French, it's cats that have poor paw control: "cat's writing." When an English speaker is having difficulty communicating because she has *a frog in her throat,* a similarly challenged Frenchman's throat contains a cat. Rather than *eat crow,* a Frenchman "swallows a toad." For French cats, being swallowed isn't all they have to worry about; when we have *other fish to fry,* the French more cruelly have "other cats to whip," and

Cleaner than a frog's armpit
Spanish: broke

when we *hem and haw,* Russians "pull the cats' tail." To say someone is forgetful or *has a head like a sieve* in Yiddish, is to call that person a "cat head." The Japanese expression "a cat defecates" seems a particularly cat-headed way of saying to "sneakily put something in your pocket." Pickpockets targeting the Japanese, beware.

When a German wants to indicate that something is important, he says "there the donkey falls." And after the donkey has fallen, the same German might "feed barley to the tail when the donkey is dead"—the equivalent of our *bolting the barn door after the horse has gotten out.** Speaking of

* The Irish/Welsh have a proverb that insightfully warns "never bolt a barn door with a boiled carrot."

expired equines, when we *beat a dead horse,* the Chinese are crueler and will "beat a drowning dog." Similarly, unforgiving Chinese "throw stones on a man who has fallen in the well." When we *let the cat out of the bag,* the Japanese "reveal the legs of a horse," the Chinese only "show the horse's hoof." As we hope to *kill two birds with one stone,* Italians "catch two pigeons with one fava bean," Germans "hit two flies with one hand clap," and Hindi speakers "get a mango at the price of a stone."

When we admonish someone for *being a chicken,* Arabs would call the same person "camel hearted." Similarly, scared Italians "have the heart of a hare," reticent Russians are told "not to be a rabbit," and timid Hindi speakers are called a "wet cat." Rather than being afraid, Italian chickens apparently aren't very bright; when an Italian says someone is "really a chicken," he means that person is easily fooled.

BIRDS

- To have a bird: *to be nuts, crazy (German)*
- Like a heavenly bird: *lead an untroubled life (Russian)*
- Walk like a golden-eyed bird: *to strut about (Russian)*
- The only thing missing is the bird's milk: *having everything under the sun (Russian)*
- To throw a chicken at oneself: *to run away (Spanish, Chile)*
- To die chicken: *to not reveal a secret (Spanish, Chile)*

Animals

- Like a perch in a chicken coop: *insulted, pooped on* (*Spanish, Mexico*)
- Chicken's eye point of view: *having limited vision* (*Yiddish*)
- Plucked out like a chicken: *done in, spent* (*Yiddish*)
- Don't be a tawny owl: *don't be stupid* (*Italian*)
- Stop being the owl: *stop flirting* (*French*)
- To carry owls to Athens: *useless* (*German*)
- An owl egg sunny-side up: *a practical joke* (*German*)
- Son of an owl: *an out-and-out fool* (*Hindi*)
- To eat owl's flesh: *to act idiotically* (*Hindi*)
- Love the house, love the crows: *love me, love my dog* (*Chinese*)
- White crow: *a rare find* (*Russian*)
- Pay for the ducks: *pay unfairly* (*Spanish, Mexico*)
- To be duck: *to be broke* (*Spanish, Peru*)
- Ducks are falling already roasted: *it's scorching hot* (*Spanish, Chile*)
- Those waiting for ducks to fall already roasted from the sky will be waiting a very long time: *proverb* (*Chinese*)
- To let a duck through: *to spread rumors* (*Russian*)
- A good duck: *someone easily fooled* (*Japanese*)
- Cold enough for ducks: *freezing cold* (*French*)
- To shoot at sparrows with cannon: *to overdo* (*German*)
- To get the partridge drunk: *to beat around the bush* (*Spanish*)
- Neither peahen nor raven: *neither fish nor fowl* (*Russian*)

Ducks are falling already roasted
Spanish: it's scorching hot

Tiger's head with a snake tail
Chinese: things that start off well but end up poorly

FELINES

- Here the cat broods: *to be suspicious (Italian)*
- He's a cat: *he's smart, clever (Italian)*
- We're four cats: *too few people for the task (Italian)*
- The cat goes to the lard so much that she loses her paw: *curiosity killed the cat (Italian)*
- There's an ugly cat to skin: *that's a big problem (Italian)*
- Fine words don't feed a cat: *talk is cheap (Italian)*
- I've got a cat in my throat: *I've got a frog in my throat (French)*
- Have other cats to whip*: *have other fish to fry (French)*

* Tangent—a habitually disobedient slave in ancient Rome was called a wearer out of whips.

- There's no reason to whip a cat: *not worth the fuss (French)*
- Don't wake the sleeping cat: *let sleeping dogs lie (French)*
- Cat's writing: *poor writing, chicken scratches (French)*
- A cat skinner: *a jerk (Spanish, Chile)*
- To give cat for rabbit: *to deceive (Spanish)*
- To bell the cat: *to do something difficult (Spanish)*
- To look for 3 or 5 feet on a cat: *the impossible (Spanish)*
- Cat weeping for the mouse: *insincere crying, crocodile tears (Chinese)*
- Trusting a cat to guard the bonito: *a fox in the henhouse, wolf among the chickens (Japanese)*
- Give gold coins to a cat: *cast pearls* before swine (Japanese)*
- A cat's forehead: *a small area (Japanese)*
- To put a cat over oneself: *to feign ignorance (Japanese)*
- A cat defecates: *to pocket something stealthily (Japanese)*
- To pull the cat's tail: *to hesitate (Russian)*
- Cat scratches on the soul: *something gnawing at one's heart (Russian)*
- A cat's leap: *a short distance (German)*
- To make a cat's laundry: *to wash superficially (German)*
- Wet cat: *timid individual (Hindi)*
- Cat head: *to be forgetful (Yiddish)*
- To buy a cat in a bag: *to buy a pig in a poke, to be cheated (German)*
- To become a tiger: *a roaring drunk (Japanese)*
- A tiger cub: *a treasure (Japanese)*
- Let a tiger return to the mountain: *store trouble for the future and/or let sleeping dogs lie (Chinese)*

---

* In Persian myth, pearls were thought to be the frozen tears of the gods.

CANINES

- Seven lives like a dog: *a cat has nine lives (Italian)*
- Stop leading the dog around the barnyard: *cut to the chase, don't beat around the bush (Italian)*
- To have some quality of a dog: *stylish (French)*
- A good dog never gets a good bone: *nice guys finish last (French)*
- Dog foot : *to wander (Spanish, Mexico)*
- Little dog of all weddings: *very social person (Spanish)*
- Do the dead dog: *leave without paying (Spanish, Chile)*
- When dogs were tied with sausages: *a very long time ago (Spanish, Uruguay)*
- Like a dog in a canoe: *to be very nervous (Spanish, Puerto Rico)*
- Beat a drowning dog: *crush an already defeated enemy (Chinese)*
- Dog-headed counselor: *a bad adviser (Chinese)*
- Like a dog and a monkey: *on bad terms (Japanese)*
- To hang all the dogs: *to blame someone else (Russian)*
- Like a fifth foot on a dog: *useless (Russian)*
- A fat dog: *a shocking piece of news (German)*
- Rain young dogs: *rain heavily (German)*
- If I speak my mother will die, if I don't my father will eat dog meat: *an acute dilemma, between a rock and a hard place (Hindi)*
- The dog's tail remains crooked: *incorrigible (Arabic)*
- A dog's fart: *nonsense (Chinese)*

- So that was the poodle's core: *that's what was behind the matter (German)*
- A dog has licked your mouth: *a mild curse (Polish)*
- Between dog and wolf: *at dusk (French)*
- Live in the butt of the wolf: *live very far away (Italian)*
- In the mouth of the wolf: *with luck (Italian)*

HORSE-LIKE ANIMALS

- Little horse style: *piggy-back (Italian)*
- Horse: *idiot (Yiddish)*
- You're on the horse: *you're all set (Yiddish)*
- To shine like a honey-cake horse: *to smile broadly (German)*
- To tell someone from a horse: *tell a tall tale (German)*
- To have a horse's foot: *a hidden disadvantage (German)*
- Show the horse's hoof: *the plot is revealed (Chinese)*
- Like a horse that grows only in the number of teeth: *having accomplished nothing despite one's advanced age (Chinese)*
- Like ten thousand horses rushing forward: *to rush in (Chinese)*
- Here the donkey falls: *there's the rub (the important part)* (Italian)
- Feeding barley to the tail when the donkey is dead: *to lock the barn door after the horse has bolted (Spanish)*
- Donkey killers: *dictionaries (Spanish, Mexico)*

A camel can't see its own hump
Arabic: a pot calling a kettle black

- Female donkey: *bus (Spanish, Guatemala)*
- Camel-hearted: *timid (Hindi)*
- I have no female or male camel in it: *not my business (Arabic)*
- To mount [one] on a mule: *to expose to disgrace (Hindi)*

- To get off the burro: *to back down, give up* (*Spanish*)
- A camel cannot see its own hump: *a pot calling a kettle black* (*Arabic*)
- On which side will the camel sit?: *let's see how things turn out* (*Hindi*)

FISH & SEA CREATURES

- Way of the fish: *law of the jungle* (*Hindi*)
- He who sleeps gets no fish: *don't be late* (*Italian*)
- To drown the fish: *to lose by deliberate confusion* (*French*)
- To change the fishes' water: *to urinate* (*Spanish, Costa Rica*)
- Scaled like a fish: *frightened or nervous* (*Spanish, Mexico*)
- Codfish: *an agreeable or lazy person* (*Spanish, Colombia*)
- Bye fish: *a comic way to say goodbye* (*Spanish*)
- Like fish in water: *in a very agreeable situation* (*Chinese*)
- To be like a fish in water: *to enjoy comforts, be in one's element* (*Spanish*)
- Climb a tree to catch a fish: *attempt the impossible* (*Chinese*)
- Knock oneself out like a fish against ice: *against all odds* (*Russian*)
- You see less than a fish through its butt: *not very bright* (*Spanish*)

Climb a tree to catch a fish
Chinese: attempt the impossible

- A guest and a fish after three days are poison: *proverb*
  (French)
- Cooked like a lobster: *exhausted (Italian)*
- An octopus in a garage: *like a fish out of water (Spanish)*
- There's an eel under the rock: *something's suspicious,*
  something's fishy (French)

OTHER ANIMALS

- Rabbit punch: *whiplash injury (French)*
- He's a famous rabbit: *he's a sly devil (French)*
- To give cat for rabbit: *to dupe (Spanish)*
- To have the heart of a rabbit: *to be fearful (Italian)*
- To know how the rabbit runs: *to know your way around (German)*
- A cow bell: *a chatter box (Russian)*
- Eviscerate a cow: *to bad mouth (Spanish, Argentina)*
- To not go on cowhide: *to be beyond belief (German)*
- Sell someone a bear: *to pull someone's leg, to tease (German)*
- To tie a bear to someone: *to tell tales (German)*
- To have a pig: *to be very lucky (German)*
- To poke at a bush and get a snake: *to have a plan that backfires (Japanese)*
- Show where crab spend winters: *show someone what is what (Russian)*
- As an elephant in a dish store: *like a bull in a china shop (Russian)*
- A dead fly: *one who appears dim-witted but takes advantage, hypocrite (Spanish)*
- A butterfly's leg: *a mild insult (Polish)*
- To have a titmouse under one's bangs: *crazy (German)*
- Think of a gorilla, then of a horse: *restless, capricious (Chinese)*

To die dressed
Spanish: an unnatural death

chapter four

APPEARANCES & HEALTH

Go out by the neck of your shirt

B Y DEFINITION, IDIOMS are deceptive … just like appear-ances can be. We have idioms to express exactly that thought: *all that glitters isn't gold, a wolf in sheep's cloth-ing, never judge a book by its cover,* and *clothes do not make the man.* Similarly, suspicious Italians say "clothes do not make the monk" and the Chinese warn us "not to judge the horse by its saddle." As we will see in Chapter Ten, however, some appearances can also be undeceptive. Ara-bic has a relevant proverb: "A book can be read from its title." That's clearly not applicable to this book.

Despite the admonitions of various proverbs, and despite the prevailing climate of oxymoronic *political correctness,* we are wired to judge people by appearances. We do it very quickly and non-consciously. Without giv-ing it a *second thought*, or a first conscious thought for that matter, we notice a person's race in a hundred milli-seconds and a person's gender in 150.[1]

Key aspects of the way we appear to others are beyond our conscious control. That's what makes them reliable as honest signals. For example, trained smile-ologists can use these uncontrollable truthful leaks to tell when a smile is genuine. They classify smiles as being either Pan American or Duchenne. Pan Ams are forced false smiles, which use only the muscles we have conscious control over, those around the mouth (contraction of zygomaticus major). Duchenne smiles, named after French neurologist Guillaume Duchenne, are the genuine kind and also involve involuntary contraction of muscles around the eyes (inferior part of orbicularis oculi lateralis), causing laugh lines or crow's feet. This action also pulls down the lateral border of the eyebrow. It's possible that the consciously controllable Pan Am muscles can push the cheek up (or, as the Japanese say, "the cheeks become loose") enough to cause crow's feet, which means smiling eyes can still lie. The Japanese demonstrate their greater facial acuity by noting that to look pleased is to "lower the outside corners of your eyes."

In an astonishing demonstration of the reliability of the connection between appearances and health, psychologists have shown how appearances can be undeceptive over several decades. A yearbook from Mills College for 1960 was analyzed to classify the genuineness of the girls' smiles (it is a girls-only school). Their progress through life was periodically monitored. It turns out that the women who genuinely smiled in that one photo decades ago were more likely to have happy lives, stable relationships, and better overall heath.[2]

Unfortunately, some of these once-reliable ways of judging appearances are now subject to *cosmetic perjury*. Our insatiable demand to recapture aspects of our youthful yearbook looks has created a huge industry dedicated to voluntarily immobilizing the involuntary muscles of our own faces. By injecting Botox, a powerful toxin, we can suppress the wrinkles that are usually reliable signals of aging. The relationship between beauty, the eye, and the beholder has been updated. Beauty is now also around the eye of the beheld. But such measures are a blunt instrument (the Germans might say "like shooting sparrows with a cannon"); they immobilize all of the related subtle facial signals, leaving the apparently newly youthful with an inhumanly flat emotional affect.

Surprisingly, such attempts to use poisons to engineer subtle false facial impressions aren't new. Seventeenth-century Venetian women used an extract of the belladonna plant to dilate their pupils. We are more strongly attracted to those who seem attracted to us, and pupil dilation is a powerful (and naturally involuntary) indicator of interest and attraction. That's how the plant that is the source of this early paralytic cosmetic got its name— *belladonna* means "beautiful lady" in Italian.[3]

... which brings us back to language and idioms on appearances and health ...

While English speakers say that someone looks *foxy*, meaning attractive or sexy, to a Spaniard "to be made

Shorter than a sparrow's nose
Russian: short

foxes" means almost the opposite, to be poorly dressed. In language teaching, these sorts of words or phrases that mean something very different when translated are called "false friends"—more on those later. When we say someone has the "face of a monkey," that typically wouldn't be a compliment, but to a Spaniard that would mean the person is cute (usually used to describe children). While a short Englishman might be *knee-high to a grasshopper,* the equivalent Russian isn't quite so diminutive, being "shorter than a sparrow's nose," and a vertically challenged Frenchman is even more impressive, being as "tall as three apples." Speaking of tall, we don't have a widely used English idiom for tallness, but such a vertically blessed Spaniard would be "taller than the hope of a poor person."

Where we might say that someone is as *strong as an ox,* a similarly powerful Spaniard would be "made into a mule." *Strong as an ox* also has the connotation of being very healthy, which in Russian is to be like "blood with milk." To achieve the same status, a Frenchman is required only to have "sound feet and eyes." At the opposite end of the health spectrum, both Russians and French who aren't well are "not in their plates." If not being well goes on too long, we might end up *with one foot in the grave,* whereas a similarly imperiled Spanish speaker would be more active, having "one foot in the stirrup." Spanish speakers apparently prefer to die naked—since for them to "die dressed" is to "die of unnatural causes." When dead we *push up daisies;* however, the recently departed French continue their love of eating: Their corpses "eat dandelions by their roots." At the same time, some deceased Germans have a decreased appetite, as they just "look at a radish from underneath," while others "bite into grass."

SKINNY

- To go out by the neck of the shirt (*Spanish*)
- To fall out of a suit (*German*)
- Thin as a breadstick or nail (*Italian*)
- To be an asparagus (*French*)
- Become like a thorn: *very thin, wasting away* (*Hindi*)

FAT

- Lots of soup or full of soup (*French*)
- Riding breeches: *to have saddlebags* (*French*)
- Juicy: *a plump attractive person* (*Yiddish*)
- Bed-breaking: *hefty* (*Hindi*)
- Ganges of dung: *a fat (also useless) person or a complete fool* (*Hindi*)

SHORT OR TALL

- Taller than the hope of a poor person (*Spanish, Puerto Rico*)
- Tall as three apples (*French*)
- Shorter than a sparrow's nose (*Russian*)
- Noodle: *a tall thin person* (*Yiddish*)

WELL DRESSED/STYLISH

- To have some quality of a dog: *to be stylish* (*French*)
- To be pulled down/drawn by four pins: *to be dressed up* (*French*)
- To be tied up: *to be very chic* (*French*)
- To put yourself on your thirty-one: *dressed to the nines* (*French*)
- Dressed in twenty-five pins: *all dressed up* (*Spanish*)

- With pipe and glove: *all dressed up (Spanish, Mexico)*
- Hair cream stallion: *dandy (German)*
- Sugar one's waffle/honeycomb: *put on makeup (French)*
- To be touched up: *to have cosmetic surgery (Italian)*
- A cleaning/to reface the façade: *a facelift (French)*

POORLY DRESSED

- Four-dollar outfit *(Italian)*
- To be made foxes *(Spanish)*
- Look like the Mona Lisa after a spanking *(Czech)*
- To look like a hanged cat: *to not look good (Danish)*

UNATTRACTIVE/UNAPPEALING

- With the head of a buck and the eyes of a rat: *proverb (Chinese)*
- To have the face of bad milk: *to look in a bad mood (Spanish)*
- To make one's face cloudy: *to look glum (Japanese)*
- A salty face: *to look sullen (Japanese)*
- Neither skin nor muzzle: *unappealing look (Russian)*
- Like the backside of a vulture: *unattractive (Finnish)*

HEALTHY/FIT/STRONG

- To be blown up like a balloon: *over muscular (Italian)*
- To be a wardrobe: *to be well built (Italian)*
- A wardrobe with a mirror: *to be well built (French)*
- A wardrobe of ice cream: *a great hulking brute (French)*
- Square: *well built (Spanish, Mexico)*
- To be made into a mule: *to be very strong (Spanish)*
- A flower pot: *a muscular pot (Spanish, Chile)*
- To be healthy like a fish *(Italian)*
- To keep the line: *to keep trim (French)*
- To have the French fry: *to be in great shape (French)*
- To have the salad: *to be fit (German)*
- Blood with milk: *picture of health (Russian)*
- To have sound feet and eyes: *to be healthy (French)*
- While one's eyes are still black: *while still healthy (Japanese)*
- Increase in fat content: *in one's prime (Japanese)*

OLD

- Onion head: *with gray hair (Spanish, Mexico)*
- To be for light soup and good wine: *on one's last legs (Spanish)*
- The bones become loose: *to be impaired by age or injury (Hindi)*
- Ripe mango: *old person (Hindi)*

- Out to plant cabbage: *out to pasture, retired, old (French)*
- Gate-closing panic: *fear of time running out (German)*

ILL / WEAK / TIRED

- Tongue hanging out like a man's tie: *exhausted (Spanish)*
- Stick one's chin out: *exhausted (Japanese)*
- Cooked like a lobster: *exhausted (Italian)*
- Plucked out like a chicken: *exhausted (Yiddish)*
- Have the midday devil: *midlife crisis (French)*
- To flip one's eyes: *faint (Italian)*
- Not in your plate: *to not feel well (French and Russian)*
- One hundred holes and one thousand wounds: *in a state of ruin (Chinese)*
- No skin no face (which rhymes in the original): *to look awful (Russian)*
- To smile yellow: *to give a sickly grin (French)*
- To loosen one's teeth: *something that is nauseating (Japanese)*
- To make the kittens: *to vomit or throw up (Italian)*
- Like the she-monkey: *under the weather (Spanish, Chile)*
- No unscratched skin on the body: *injured all over (Hindi)*
- The wound of words is worse than the wound of swords: *proverb (Arabic)*

- May all your teeth but one fall out and may that get a toothache: *curse (Yiddish)**

DYING/DEAD

- To have one foot in the stirrup: *to be at death's door (Spanish, Mexico)*
- Two fingers from death: *at death's door (French)*
- To whistle on the last hole: *to be at death's door (German)*
- An insect's breathing: *at death's door (Japanese)*
- The heart to be in the throat: *at death's door (Hindi)*
- The nails to be blue: *at death's door (Hindi)*
- To die dressed: *to die unnaturally (Spanish, Mexico)*
- To pass one's weapon to the left: *to die (French)*
- To swallow one's birth certificate: *to die (French)*
- To eat dandelions by their roots: *to be pushing up daisies (French)*
- To look at a radish from underneath: *to be pushing up daisies (German)*
- To break your pipe: *to die (French)*
- To close the umbrella: *to die (Spanish, Costa Rica)*
- To hang up one's saber: *to die (Spanish, Cuba)*
- To hang up the gloves: *to die (Spanish)*
- To scare off the mule: *to die (Spanish, Mexico)*
- To become a Buddha: *to die (Japanese)*
- To stretch out the legs: *to die (Hindi)*

---

* In a similar vein, the Dutch have a curse: "May you get cancer behind your heart, so a doctor can't reach it."

- Dissolution of the body into its five constituents: *to die (Hindi)*
- Quiet ones: *the dead (Spanish, Colombia)*
- Who knows when death or a customer will come: *proverb (India)*
- Go into the ground: *drop dead (Yiddish)*
- On whom mercy is shown: *the deceased, the late (Hindi)*
- The bald one: *death (Spanish, Cuba)*
- Flesh of the dead: *mushroom (Spanish, Mexico)*
- He should marry the daughter of the Angel of Death: *curse (Yiddish)*

Two fingers from death
French: at death's door, almost dead

To fart higher than your butt
French: to be snooty, posh, to put on airs

chapter five

HEADS & TAILS

Pull the hair out of someone's nostrils

CROSS-CULTURAL ANATOMICAL ASSOCIATIONS can be astonishing! They can show how differently being human can be embodied in other cultures. We think of the heart as being the seat of our emotions, our true feelings, and our deepest desires; hence English expressions like *take it to heart* or *in one's heart of hearts*. The location of such seats, however, has not always been fixed.

Aristotle, considered the first serious anatomist of the West, believed the heart was the seat of thought as well as emotion. He also believed the brain was a radiator. He backed into that view from the observation that we are less hot blooded, less easily provoked, and less emotional in our responses than other animals. Fundamentally his *seat of the pants* logic* was that something had to be cooling our blood ... and he apparently didn't think we were using our larger brains for anything else. He is also reputed to have *sown the seeds* of the hegemony of reason. He believed that humans are fundamentally

---

* *Revealed in his book* Posterior Analytics *(with the benefit of hindsight, that's funnier than intended).*

rational beings and that was what distinguished us from animals. Galen, the renowned Graeco-Roman physician, moved the seat of reason to the brain, but he differentiated between the heart as responsible for emotions, and the liver as the source of passions.

In stark contrast, the Japanese think of the stomach area as the place where their true feelings and intentions lie. References to similar sentiments survive in our language, for example in phrases like *gut feeling* and *gut instinct*. While we downplay our intestinal intelligence, the Japanese are far more interested in (pre-mortem*) gut reading. And it's not just their own; they're interested in gathering intelligence on the state of the intestines of others. They prefer visible viscera. When the Japanese say "your belly is transparent," it means that you are not hiding anything, your true intentions are clear. Hence when the Japanese say "there is something in their bellies," they don't mean they have eaten; they mean they have *something up their sleeve*. Where we *set our minds (or hearts)* on something, an equally resolute Japanese would "tighten his belly." If we don't achieve what we had set our hearts on, we might be *brokenhearted*, whereas, to keep up the consistency of anatomical displacement, a similarly afflicted Japanese's "intestines are torn." Being heartbroken we might need to unburden ourselves, whereas a Japanese would "open up his liver and gall." When we finally learn the inevitable lessons of

---

* *In contrast to a long history of postmortem entrail reading as practiced on sacrificial animals.*

disappointment *by taking something to heart,* the Japanese more alarmingly "chisel it into their livers"!

Languages can be windows into the workings of minds. Neuroscientists now have new windows to look through. High-tech tools can probe the physical underpinnings of our mental lives ... including how we process language. Though some of these tools are still quite crude, almost a sort of high-tech internal phrenology, they nevertheless are yielding impressive results. We have long known which parts of the brain are required for language processing in general—Broca's area and Wernicke's area, both of which are usually located on the left side of the brain. This gross neuro-anatomy was discovered using older techniques of brain-damage-ology. The newer tools are able to inspect much finer levels of detail of language processing. Scientists are beginning to identify how the brain encodes the meanings of some words, e.g., they believe that verbs and nouns are stored in separate ways. It seems that concrete nouns are encoded in areas of the brain used to sense or manipulate the referent objects, which is leading to a theory of meaning based on function.[1] fMRI (functional magnetic resonance image) scanning has been used to watch how listeners' brains try to predict the meaning of words as soon as they have heard the first syllable.[2] Scientists have been able to watch as the brain nonconsciously considers many possible meanings of words, before it has even heard the final syllable.

It's probably this sort of prediction and resulting potential for semantic ambush that attracts us to novelty in language. Shakespeare knew all about that. Philip Davis, a literature professor, and Neil Roberts, a neuroscientist, are collaborating to use brain-scanning tools to show how particular kinds of novel language constructs can excite us. In *Shakespeare Thinking,* Davis reports on the effect of "functional shift" or word-class conversion.[3] Though conservative word-watchers bemoan such conversions (verb-ification or noun-ification), they have been going on for centuries. And one of the greatest practitioners was Shakespeare. For example: "spaniell'd me" (*Anthony and Cleopatra*) or "this day shall gentle his condition" (*Henry V*). Davis says, "While the Shakespearian functional shift was semantically integrated with ease, it triggered a syntactic re-evaluation process likely to raise attention." In other words, we could easily understand what Shakespeare meant, but his use of slippery syntax forced us to pay more attention. Brain measurements, using EEG (electroencephalogram), have been able to demonstrate that these functional shifts are measurably more stimulating than just plain old semantic novelty.[4]

Davis also notes the "closeness of functional shift to metaphor" and goes on to describe it as "that characteristic mental conversion that Shakespeare so loved." Some of Shakespeare's functional shifts were highly compressed and therefore more potent metaphors; "spaniell'd me," for example, is a highly compressed form of "followed at my heels like a spaniel." That makes me wonder about the closeness of the relationship between metaphors and idioms and the shift they require.

Neuro-linguists are using their new high-tech tools to look carefully into idiom processing and comprehension. A look at the titles of some recent papers reveals the state of the art:

"Left but Not Right Temporal Involvement in Opaque Idiom Comprehension," 2004.

"Evidence of Bilateral Involvement in Idiom Comprehension, an fMRI Study," 2007.

"Idiom Comprehension: A Prefrontal Task?" 2008.[5]

Though the *jury is still out* on the specifics, it's clear that idiom comprehension involves more of the brain than processing the equivalent purely literal phrase. And though I haven't found any research specifically on functional shiftiness and idioms, I don't think it's too much of a stretch to draw an analogy between the two and in so doing perhaps partially explain the enduring popularity of idioms.

Further phrenological findings show that, since written Chinese is pictographic rather than alphabetic, the Chinese use different parts of their brains to read. Maryanne Wolf reports on this in her fascinating book on the history of reading, *Proust and the Squid*. She also points out that reading is evolutionarily a very recent activity. And thus it's highly unnatural. We have no neuro-biological systems that have evolved expressly to support the deciphering of the frozen outpourings of other minds. You are at this precise moment engaged in one of the miracles of brain plasticity—reading. Wolf also points out another remarkable aspect of reading, which she summarizes using Proust's elegant prose: You and I are both engaged in "that fruitful miracle of communicating in the midst of solitude."[6]

Getting back to more general anatomical astonishments—it's not just the insides of Japanese midriffs that seem more important than ours. While for us *navel gazing* isn't to be recommended, it seems watching Japanese navels could be much more useful and entertaining. The Japanese, when they regret something deeply, "gnaw on their own navels." When sulking they "twist their navels." But that's the least of their navel talents—when indicating something is laughable, they accuse one another of "making tea with their navels." A Yiddish speaker can insult you by telling you that "onions should grow in your navel." In one part of South Africa a common greeting among Xhosa speakers consists in asking "where is your navel," which is their way of asking where you are from. It refers to the practice of burying the placenta of a newborn at the doorway of its family's house. Hindi has a similar idiom.

Okay, enough *navel gazing* and on to other body parts …

I swear *I'm not pulling your leg* or, as the Russians would say, "I'm not hanging noodles on your ears."

A similar protestation for a German would be to "let a bear loose on someone," and for a Spaniard to "grab someone's hair." A Japanese who wanted to dupe someone would more specifically "pull the hair out of their nostrils." Meanwhile, "hanging something from your nose" in Japan means to be vain. To dupe someone in Czech is, alarmingly, to "hang balls on his nose." Curiously, a Yiddish speaker needs a *hole in the head* like she needs a "lung and liver on her nose." Whereas we *split hairs,* the French are more exacting; they "cut a hair in four."

As noted above, the Japanese have particularly talented anatomies. When they want something badly, they say it's "like a hand coming out of one's throat." When gasping for breath one "breathes through his shoulder." An enterprising Arab seizes an opportunity by knowing "where to bite the shoulder." A Russian who "bites the elbow" is *crying over spilt milk.* To try to charm someone, the Japanese "speak through the nose." And when they have something on their minds, i.e., they are concerned, they "make their eyebrows cloudy." Sometimes the Japanese have good reason to have cloudy eyebrows; when something bad comes to light they say, "one's buttocks split."

Speaking of the hind area, when we say someone is a *brown-noser* or *butt kisser,* similarly servile Italians are "foot-lickers." Equivalent Hindi speakers more specifically "lick the soles of the feet" (they have a related expression that translates as "foot nectar," meaning "water in which the feet of an idol or of a respected personage have been washed"). A groveling Russian, *on the other hand*, "licks eye," whereas a submissive Spaniard would be a "belly with calluses." The Japanese expression for a toady is excrementally evocative; it literally means "goldfish poop."

Enough preamble; let's get into the heart (and belly) of the wonderful world of anatomical idioms, starting from the top:

HEAD & NECK & HAIR

- To grab someone's hair: *to pull someone's leg (Spanish)*
- To let one's hair grow white in the sun: *to idle one's life away (Hindi)*
- The coat of hair is good: *to be from a good family (Japanese)*
- To bend the spiral of hair on the crown of one's head: *to become nasty (Japanese)*
- To devour hair from head: *to eat one out of house and home (German)*
- Anger hair points to heaven: *to be livid, hopping mad (Japanese)*
- Not to leave a hair on one's head: *to beat soundly (Hindi)*
- Feeling that hair on the back of head is pulled back: *reluctantly (Japanese)*
- A single hair from nine oxen: *a drop in a bucket (Chinese)*

- To cut a hair in four: *to split hairs (French)*
- To pull the hair out of someone's nostrils: *to dupe someone (Japanese)*
- Smoke belches from the seven openings on the head: *very angry (Chinese)*
- To squeeze one's head: *to rack one's brain (Japanese)*
- To eat the brain of: *to bore with chatter (Hindi)*
- To empty the brain: *to tire oneself by talking too much (Hindi)*
- Good health on your head: *be well (Yiddish)*
- Go twist your own head: *go fly a kite (Yiddish)*
- You're climbing on my head: *you're getting on my nerves (Arabic)*
- A two-headed woman: *a pregnant woman (Hindi)*
- A neck doesn't turn: *heavily in debt (Japanese)*
- To ride on the neck: *to dominate (Hindi)*
- Get your jaw dislocated: *die laughing (Japanese)*

FACE

- What is written on the brow: *destiny (Hindi)*
- To notch in the forehead: *to commit to memory, to remember well (Russian)*
- Forehead to forehead: *face to face (Russian)*
- Seven inches in a forehead: *as wise as Solomon (Russian)*
- To puff up cheeks: *to gossip (Spanish, Chile)*
- The face to be noseless: *without shame (Hindi)*

- A face full of spring air: *radiant with happiness (Chinese)*
- A stepmother's face: *an unsmiling face, a sullen look (Chinese)*
- To make one's face cloudy: *to look glum (Japanese)*
- A salty face: *a sullen face (Japanese)*
- A flame comes out of one's face: *blush (Japanese)*
- Have the face of fixed cement: *have a lot of nerve (Spanish)*
- To suck with the face down: *to be silly, ignorant (Hindi)*
- Take by the chin: *coax, appease (Hindi)*
- To be left with the square face: *to be very surprised (Spanish, Mexico)*
- To use someone with one's chin: *to order someone around (Japanese)*
- To stick one's chin out: *to become exhausted (Japanese)*

EYES

- Flames licking at one's eyebrows: *a desperate situation (Chinese)*
- Urgent like eyebrows on fire: *extremely urgent (Chinese)*
- With dancing eyebrows and a radiant face: *enraptured (Chinese)*
- Something that causes one to put saliva on one's eyebrows: *a fake (Japanese)*
- To put saliva on one's eyebrows: *to take with a grain of salt (Japanese)*

- To open knitted brows: *to breathe freely again* (*Japanese*)
- Hit not the eyebrow but right in the eye: *hit the nail on the head* (*Russian*)
- To make one's eyebrows cloudy: *to be concerned* (*Japanese*)
- To burn one's eyebrows: *to study hard* (*Spanish*)
- The curtains: *the eyelids* (*Spanish, Cuba*)
- To throw powder in your eyes: *to kid yourself* (*French*)
- To lick eye: *to kiss up* (*Spanish, Puerto Rico*)
- To be a piece of meat with eyes: *to be useless* (*Spanish, Dominican Republic*)
- Eyes without pupils: *look but not see* (*Chinese*)
- To change one's eye color: *to have a serious look* (*Japanese*)
- While one's eyes are still black: *while alive* (*Japanese*)
- To get one's eyes stolen: *to be dazzled* (*Japanese*)
- To lower the outside corners of one's eyes: *to be pleased* (*Japanese*)
- To make the outside corners of one's eyes stand up: *to nitpick* (*Japanese*)
- To look at someone with white eyes: *to look at someone disdainfully* (*Japanese*)
- To bring four eyes together: *to meet the glance* (*Hindi*)
- Poison for one's eyes: *too much of a temptation* (*Japanese*)
- To throw an eye at: *to guard, to mind* (*Yiddish*)

EARS

- To lower the ears: *to give in, in a dispute* (*Spanish*)
- To flatten the ear: *to sleep* (*Spanish, Mexico*)
- To iron one's ear: *to go to sleep* (*Spanish*)
- To have fallen ears: *to be crestfallen* (*Spanish*)
- Water into the ear of someone sleeping: *a shock* (*Japanese*)
- Ear-nectar: *a sweet voice or sound* (*Hindi*)
- Hearing test: *call with nothing to say* (*Russian*)
- I'm not hanging noodles on your ears: *I'm not pulling your leg* (*Russian*)
- To warm somebody's ear: *to chastise* (*French*)
- Like a Volkswagen with doors open: *having big ears* (*Spanish*)

NOSE

- A fly on the nose: *a chip on the shoulder* (*Italian*)
- Soldering iron: *a big nose* (*French*)
- He doesn't wipe his nose with his foot: *he has ideas above his station* (*French*)
- Like a lung and liver on my nose: *like a hole in the head* (*Yiddish*)
- To break someone's nose: *to discourage* (*Japanese*)
- To hang something on one's nose: *to be vain* (*Japanese*)

I'm not hanging noodles on your ears
Russian: I'm not pulling your leg

- To speak through the nose: *to sweet talk (Japanese)*
- To speak through the nose: *to double talk (Yiddish)*
- A wax-nose: *one who changes opinions easily (Hindi)*
- To make one's own nose taller: *to boast (Japanese)*
- Bring one's nose against someone's: *face to face (Japanese)*
- To make nose medicine effective: *to bribe (Japanese)*
- Earn oneself a golden nose: *make a lot of money (German)*
- Having the nose cut off: *to be in disgrace (Hindi)*
- To take off the nose ring: *to become a widow (Hindi)*
- A hair of the nose: *respected, honored (Hindi)*
- To keep one's nose: *to keep one's honor (Hindi)*
- Move the wings of one's nose incessantly: *have a swelled head (Japanese)*
- With eyes and nose attached: *almost complete (Japanese)*
- The line of the nose: *straight as an arrow (Hindi)*
- You got your nose burned: *you had your leg pulled (Persian)*
- To pull the worms out of the nose: *to tell all (German)*
- To pull the hair out of someone's nostrils: *to dupe someone (Japanese)*

MOUTH & TEETH

- At the flower of the lip: *on the tip of the tongue (Spanish, Latin America)*
- Three inches of a tongue: *glib tongue, sweet talk (Japanese)*

- A cat's tongue: *to be sensitive to heat (Japanese)*
- To use two tongues: *to tell a lie (Japanese)*
- Have a well-hung tongue: *to be eloquent (French)*
- Long tongue: *says too much (Spanish)*
- Long-tongued: *impudent, abusive (Hindi)*
- Box of lies: *the mouth (French)*
- Have potatoes in the mouth: *speak unclearly (Spanish, Chile)*
- Honey-mouthed and dagger-hearted: *hypocritical (Chinese)*
- To produce wind at the corners of one's mouth: *to be eloquent (Chinese)*
- To have a hard tooth: *to have a sharp tongue (French)*
- To loosen one's teeth: *something that's nauseating (Japanese)*
- To not put clothes on one's teeth: *to tell it like it is (Japanese)*
- One's teeth itch: *one feels important (Japanese)*
- Itchy teeth: *gossip (Russian)*
- To break teeth: *be ruined (Russian)*
- Have a tooth: *hold a grudge (Russian)*
- To seize the moon by the teeth: *to try to do the impossible (French)*
- Feigned laughter ruins the teeth: *proverb (India)*
- Having neither innards nor teeth: *a very poor person (Hindi)*
- A tooth gift: *a love bite (Hindi)*

CHEST

- At pure lung: *working very hard (Spanish, Latin America)*
- One's breast is deep: *big-hearted (Japanese)*
- One's chest bounces: *to get excited (Japanese)*
- Make one's chest jump: *to be excited (Japanese)*
- Having the breast torn: *to be grieving (Hindi)*
- Something floats in one's chest: *something crosses one's mind (Japanese)*
- To bend one's chest backward: *to take pride in (Japanese)*
- Won't fit in one's chest: *weighing on one's mind (Spanish)*
- Attack my lung: *give me a cigarette (Spanish, Mexico)*

STOMACH/TORSO/MIDRIFF/BACK

- To give of stomach: *to throw up (Italian)*
- To have liver: *to have heart (Italian)*
- To have livers: *to have cold feet (French)*
- Open up one's liver and gall: *unburden oneself (Japanese)*
- Chisel something into one's liver: *take something to heart (Japanese)*
- One's liver is extracted: *dumbfounded (Japanese)*
- To be a liver: *to be a pain, a jerk (Spanish, Mexico)*
- To have kidneys: *to be brave (Spanish)*
- Belly with calluses: *a sycophant (Spanish, Chile)*
- Belly of a seal: *a sycophant (Spanish, Chile)*

- One's belly is ready: *to be resolved (Japanese)*
- One's belly balloons: *to get frustrated (Japanese)*
- One's belly is thick: *big-hearted (Japanese)*
- One's belly gets cured: *to calm down (Japanese)*
- One's belly is black: *to be deceitful (Japanese)*
- One's belly is rotten: *to be despicable (Japanese)*
- One's belly is transparent: *to have clear intentions (Japanese)*
- One's belly boils over: *to be furious (Japanese)*
- There's something in someone's belly: *an ulterior motive (Japanese)*
- To cure one's belly: *to get revenge (Japanese)*
- To tighten one's belly: *to be resolved (Japanese)*
- To see through someone's belly: *to read someone's mind (Japanese)*
- To search someone's belly: *to feel someone out (Japanese)*
- In the chaos of a belly standing up: *an angry fit (Japanese)*
- Mercury in one's belly: *ants in one's pants (German)*
- Black-bellied: *wicked, evil (Japanese)*
- Broken-bellied: *starving (Hindi)*
- One's stomach skin is distorted: *to die laughing (Japanese)*
- To sink the stomach: *to suffer indigestion (Hindi)*
- Like the bowels being removed: *numb (Japanese)*
- One's intestines are torn: *heartbroken (Japanese)*
- One's intestines are rotten: *morally corrupt (Japanese)*
- With all entrails: *everything included (Russian)*
- Stomach-fire: *the digestion (Hindi)*
- To feel a throb around the ribs: *an omen of a friend's visit (Hindi)*

- Bury an umbilical cord: *a hereditary claim on land* (*Hindi*)
- To scratch someone's back: *to outsmart* (*Japanese*)
- Get with one's own hump: *by the sweat of one's brow* (*Russian*)
- Only the grave can fix a hump: *a leopard can't change its spots* (*Russian*)
- Make backbone and ribs one: *beat unmercifully* (*Hindi*)
- Show one's back: *reveal a weak point* (*Japanese*)

NAVELS

- I'll make tea with my navel: *don't make me laugh, don't pull my leg* (*Japanese*)
- One's navel boils tea: *it's laughable* (*Japanese*)
- To twist one's navel: *to sulk* (*Japanese*)
- A twisted navel: *a pervert* (*Japanese*)
- Bent belly button: *a cantankerous person* (*Japanese*)
- To gnaw one's own navel: *to regret something deeply* (*Japanese*)
- To harden one's own navel: *to be resolved* (*Japanese*)
- Many thanks in your belly button: *thanks for nothing* (*Yiddish*)
- Onions should grow from your navel: *an insult* (*Yiddish*)
- The navel of the world: *the hub of the universe* (*German*)
- Good health to your belly button: *thanks for the small favor* (*Yiddish*)

To pull up the bottom of one's kimono to reveal the buttocks
Japanese: to maintain a defiant attitude

BUTTS*

- Wet one's butt in: *get deeply involved (Spanish)*
- To grasp someone's tail: *to obtain evidence (Japanese)*
- To have light buttocks: *to be rash, not careful (Japanese)*
- To have heavy buttocks: *to be slow to act (Japanese)*
- One's bottom is stretching: *to stay too long (Japanese)*
- One's buttocks split: *to bring something bad to light (Japanese)*
- One's bottom catches fire: *time is running out (Japanese)*

* *Shakespeare used the wonderfully apt word* blindcheeks.

To light one's fingernail
Japanese: to lead a frugal life

- Pull up one's kimono to reveal buttocks: *to maintain a defiant attitude (Japanese)*
- Pot with a rounded bottom: *an undependable person (Hindi)*
- To have a butt fringed with noodles: *to be very lucky (French)*
- To wiggle your bucket: *to dance (Spanish, Mexico)*
- May a pine tree grow out of your butt: *curse (Portuguese)*
- To make a little perfume*: *to break wind (Italian)*
- A river imp's fart: *something that's easy (Japanese)*
- He squirms like a fart in a foggy soup: *he's bewildered (Yiddish)*
- To fart higher than your butt: *to be snooty, posh, put on airs (French)*

---

* Perfume originally meant "through smoke."

ARMS/HANDS/SHOULDERS

- To breathe through one's shoulder: *to gasp for breath* (*Japanese*)
- Knows where to bite the shoulder: *can seize an opportunity* (*Arabic*)
- Shoulders to be peeled: *to be very crowded* (*Hindi*)
- To look on over one's shoulder: *to look down on* (*German*)
- From the stranger's shoulder: *used clothing* (*Russian*)
- To be the armpit* of confidence: *trust completely* (*Spanish, Nicaragua*)
- To dig in one's elbows: *to study hard* (*Spanish*)
- To bite the elbow: *to cry over split milk* (*Russian*)
- To talk even through the elbows: *to be a chatterbox* (*Spanish*)
- Like a hand coming out of one's throat: *a yearning* (*Japanese*)
- One whose hands are fast: *a womanizer* (*Japanese*)
- One's hands get empty: *to have time on one's hands* (*Japanese*)
- With a hand kiss: *with the greatest pleasure* (*German*)
- To handle with salted hands: *to raise with tender care* (*Japanese*)
- Look through the fingers: *turn a blind eye* (*Russian*)
- Hide between the fingers: *to steal, to pilfer* (*Hindi*)
- Show the thumb: *a contemptuous gesture* (*Hindi*)
- Brew the dirt from someone's fingernails and drink it: *to learn a bitter lesson from someone* (*Japanese*)

---

* *Ancient Romans had armpit pluckers, often slaves, at public baths.*

- To be fingernail and dirt: *tight friends (Spanish, Mexico)*
- To burn on one's nails: *urgent (German)*
- To light one's fingernail: *to lead a frugal life (Japanese)*
- To have blue nails: *to be near death (Hindi)*

LEGS & FEET

- To be someone's leg: *dating (Spanish, Chile)*
- Stretch your legs the length of your carpet: *live within your means (Arabic)*
- One's legs stick out: *exceeding one's budget or income (Japanese)*
- Are you standing on one leg?: *Are you in a hurry? (Yiddish)*
- Be on a short leg: *on friendly terms (Russian)*
- To reveal the legs of a horse: *to show one's true colors (Japanese)*
- One's hips are gone: *to be a coward (Japanese)*
- To clap the palms on the thighs: *to challenge or prepare to fight (Hindi)*
- Press under the thigh: *keep under control (Hindi)*
- To mingle each other's knees: *an intimate talk (Japanese)*
- To get knee to knee: *an intimate talk (Japanese)*
- My knees are laughing: *to be unsteady (Japanese)*
- Gnaw one's parent's shin: *sponge off one's parent (Japanese)*
- To step on the same spot with the second foot: *to hesitate (Japanese)*

To write with the feet

Italian: to have poor penmanship

- Foot-licker: *a sycophant (Italian)*
- To write with the feet: *to have poor penmanship (Italian)*
- To live on a wide foot: *to live in grand style (Russian)*
- To live on a large foot: *in grand style (German)*
- Foot nectar: *water from washing the feet of a respected person (Hindi)*
- To lick the soles of the feet of: *to ingratiate oneself (Hindi)*
- To look at someone's feet: *to take unfair advantage of a weakness (Japanese)*
- To throw a foot: *to shake a leg, to dance (Spanish, Cuba)*

Visiting Mr. Rock
Spanish: to urinate

- Feet, why do I love you?: *said when fleeing danger*
  (Spanish, Mexico)
- Apply henna to the feet: *be reluctant to go anywhere,*
  or do anything (Hindi)
- To worship the left foot of someone: *to acknowledge*
  someone's superiority (Hindi)

OTHER IDIOMS INVOLVING BODIES
AND BODY PARTS AND BODILY FUNCTIONS

- To take off one's own skin: *to give someone some help*
  (Japanese)
- One's blood makes noise: *to get excited (Japanese)*

- A feeling of vomiting blood: *being very determined* (*Japanese*)
- To turn blood white: *to grow cold or indifferent* (*Hindi*)
- Like blood-cupping on a dead body: *useless, futile* (*Yiddish*)
- Insect acid runs through one's body: *the creeps* (*Japanese*)
- To change the fishes' water: *to urinate* (*Spanish, Costa Rica*)
- To visit Mr. Rock: *to urinate* (*Spanish*)
- Go defecate in the ocean: *Get lost!* (*Yiddish*)
- Baloney: *acronym for "bothering someone's balls for no reason"* (*Hebrew*)
- To de-testicle: *to ruin, mess up* (*Spanish, Mexico*)
- A spot for crying: *a weakness* (*Japanese*)
- Not blow in one's own moustache: *not give a damn* (*Russian*)
- Pluck the moustaches of: *to teach a painful lesson, to humble* (*Hindi*)

Stinking hair
Japanese: foreigner

chapter six

COUNTRIES

Oranges to China

NOT ALL HUMANKIND is our kind. Unkind though the thought may be, us-ness and them-ness is baked into us. And you guessed it; language can tell us how basic those base instincts are. Psychologists now have language lenses that can peer deeply into what we feel about those we don't consider our peers.

Implicit Association Tests* can explicitly measure the strength of our associations with positive and negative language and our non-conscious views of members of other groups (genders, races, nationalities, etc.). Each test involves sorting a set of words or pictures into one of two categories, as quickly as possible. The test measures the average time it takes, down to the millisecond level. Words that go against the grain of your implicit associations will take longer to access and will hence be slower to classify, and vice versa. That's just startling (or, as the Germans might say "knocks the strongest Inuit from the sled"). These tests have now been taken by millions of people, and the news

---

* You can take the Implicit Association Tests yourself at www.implicit.harvard.edu.

isn't very *politically correct*. The results show that most people have some race, gender, and age-related biases—even *PC* types who think of themselves as not harboring any biases. This sort of group identification is another example of an evolved characteristic that no longer has adaptive benefit.

Whatever your implicit views of foreigners, the explicit purpose of this book is to provide easy access to some of the wonders of their languages. In his great book on the history of English, *The Secret Life of Words*, Henry Hitchings also *dips his toe* into issues of language leakiness. He quotes the views of a 16th-century French poet who believed that language could only be improved by the "artifice and industry of men" and hence that it was our duty to ennoble our own tongue with the "ornament and excellence of other languages."[1] Hitchings also quotes a slightly later Englishman who wrote "the most renowned of other nations have entrusted [England] with the rarest Jewelles of their lipps perfection."

The English seem to have responded to that call admirably, having welcomed linguistic jewels from 350 languages. David Crystal in *Words, Words, Words* reports that only 20 percent of English's current word stock comes from Olde Englishe.[2] The rest are new coinages or the linguistic coin of other realms. Bill Bryson in his magnificent survey *The Mother Tongue* notes that this mélange has left English with richer lexical resources, having around 200,000 words in common usage, as compared to 180,000 in German and a relatively impoverished if comparatively purer 100,000[3] in French. I'm hoping that this book can, in a small way, contribute to the wholesale jewel thievery that has characterized the progress of English. Perhaps one or two of these *new-to-you* stock phrases may *strike you* as worthy of inclusion in your own word stock.

All un-isolated languages are a *melting-pot-luck* of ingredients of the choicest and catch-iest kinds. This kind of language sharing has been going on for as long as peoples of different tongues have been coming across each other. Frequently, though, the sharing hasn't always been so entirely kind. As Hitchings puts it, language mixing is often a result of "one culture chafing against another." This cultural chafing has often been extreme, involving war and conquest. English still bears the scars of its many skirmishes. That "sk" pairing came with the Nordic raiders and has stayed. As Hitchings also points out, sometimes language change has involved conquests of a different sort: "Nothing more urgently accelerates the need to communicate than" romantic desire.

As will be evident from the idiom lists in this book, different languages have different personalities. Nicholas Ostler, in his exuberantly erudite and encyclopedic language history, *Empires of the Word,* says: "Each language has its own color and flavor ... we have glimpsed some of the distinctive traits: Arabic's austere grandeur and egalitarianism; Chinese and Egyptian's unshakeable self-regard; Sanskrit's luxuriating classifications and hierarchies; Greek's self-confident innovation leading to self-obsession and pedantry; Latin's civic sense;

Spanish's rigidity, cupidity and fidelity; French's admiration of rationality; and English's admiration of business acumen."[4] As noted earlier, some believe English has a particular comic richness. Others have noted that English is heavy on downtoners—words that soften the meanings of surrounding words—enabling greater use of indirectness.

The Japanese take indirectness to very much further fields. Howard Rheingold in his exquisite book, *They Have a Word For It,* mentions a word expressing exactly that.[5] Haragei means "visceral, indirect, largely non verbal communication." Which he describes further as, "Direct verbal communication the way we use it in the West is generally shunned. Nuances, silences, gestures, facial expression are much more important.... One Japanese can understand what another is trying to communicate by closely observing posture, facial expressions, the length and timing of silences, and the various 'meaningless' sounds uttered by the other person."

Before delving into the use of country references in idioms, I need again to apologize in advance and ask you *not to shoot the messenger*. Many of the following idioms involving countries and peoples express negative stereotypes. So I'll omit further commentary. However, before getting into the lists, I will mention one stereotype that the French have, captured in their expression "to be from Birmingham. This hits close to home, since I grew up near there. It means to be utterly boring. Just to be clear that "Birmingham" is in England, not Alabama.

ON INCOMPREHENSION: AS WE WOULD SAY, IT'S ALL GREEK TO ME ...

- For me this is Arabic: *incomprehensible (Italian)*
- It's Chinese: *incomprehensible (French)*
- In Chinese: *incomprehensible (Spanish)*
- Chinese grammar: *incomprehensible (Russian)*
- I only understand train station: *incomprehensible (German)*
- All I hear is the word salad: *incomprehensible (German)*

SPEAKING OF GREEKS...

- To do the Greek: *to cheat, be a card shark (French)*
- To do the Indian: *to steal (Italian)*
- To English someone: *to fleece, trick, steal from (French)*
- Person from the Sultan's tent [moor]: *liar (Spanish, Venezuela)*
- Person from Morocco: *a lie, con, scam (Spanish, Venezuela)*
- Chinese story: *big lie, fishy story (Spanish, Mexico)*
- To build a Turk: *to make up phony stories (German)*
- To Caribbean: *to dupe (Spanish, Venezuela)*
- Perfidious Albion: *untrustworthy (French)*

AT THE OTHER END OF THE SCALES OF JUSTICE – TO BE FAIR OR EVENHANDED

- Go Roman: *go Dutch, split evenly (Italian)*
- American style: *go Dutch (Spanish, Mexico)*
- To make separate cash registers: *to go Dutch (German)*

OTHER COUNTRY & PEOPLE IDIOMS

- Golden country: *United States of America (Yiddish)*
- To discover America: *say something obvious (Italian and Russian)*
- American auction: *a Dutch auction (Flanders, Belgium)*
- Swedish curtains: *jail bars [Swedes make good steel] (German)*
- To be the Scottish shower: *to blow hot and cold (Spanish)*
- To sweat Chinese ink: *to work very hard (Spanish)*
- That knocks the strongest Eskimo from the sled: *it's too much (German)*
- Oranges from China: *no way, nothing doing (Spanish)*
- Grandma's summer: *Indian summer (Russian)*
- A cad can't become a Polish landowner: *a leopard can't change its spots (Russian)*
- English key: *monkey wrench (Spanish)*

- The land of the roast beefs: *England (French)*
- To take English leave: *to take unauthorized time off (French)*
- To take a French leave: *to go without saying goodbye (Spanish)*
- To be drunk as an English sailor: *to be completely drunk (Italian)*
- To drink like a Cossack: *to be drunk (Spanish)*
- To do the Portuguese: *to avoid paying (Italian)*
- A German argument: *quarrel for no good reason (French)*
- To be a Bedouin: *to be unsophisticated (Italian)*
- To swear like a Turk: *to swear a blue streak (Italian)*
- In the Turkish style: *rudely (French)*
- Turk's head: *scapegoat or fall guy (Spanish)*
- To be as strong as a Turk: *to be strong as an ox (French)*
- Play the Indian: *play the fool (Spanish)*
- Play the Swede: *play dumb (Spanish)*
- Stinking hair: *foreigner (Japanese)*
- Big polenta eater: *Northern Italian (Italian)*
- Big dirt guy, peasant: *Southern Italian (Italian)*
- To speak French like a Spanish cow: *to speak with a poor accent (French)*
- A pimple: *Hungarian (Czech)*
- Cockroach: *Frenchman (German)*
- Lice: *Spaniards (French)*
- The French disease: *syphilis (Italian)*

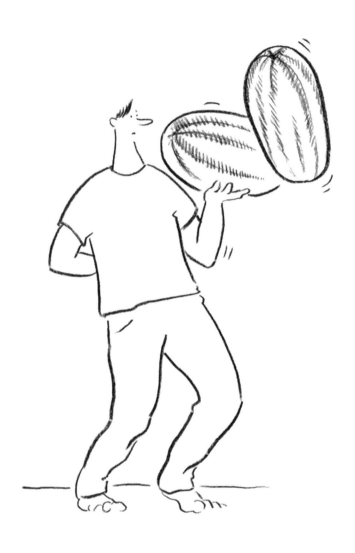

One hand cannot hold two watermelons

Iranian: one thing at a time

chapter seven

NUMBERS

The twenty-two misfortunes

T HE WAY WE THINK OF NUMBERS just doesn't add up. I'm assuming you, like me, would have a hard time imagining a world without numbers. Well, scientists (and now you) no longer have to imagine. Edward Gibson, an MIT professor of brain and cognitive sciences, has published a study on the Piraha, who live in remote northwestern Brazil. They are the first culture encountered that doesn't seem to have labels for any specific numbers.[1] Other cultures are known that are thought to have labels for only a few small numbers (perhaps up to three) and then a general label for many.* The Piraha were thought to be in this category; however, it turns out they only have a way to express relative quantities such as "some" and "more" but not to define precise numbers. Their culture just hasn't found exact numbers or counting to be useful in their environment.

Also difficult to imagine is that we are not alone in

* *Some aspect of this distinction might survive in English's number grammar—first, second, third, then everything from there ends in "th" (fourth, fifth, etc.).*

being able to do basic math. As Jim Holt reported in a *New Yorker* article, "The Numbers Guy,"[2] researchers have shown that the understanding of small specific numbers isn't restricted to guy-kind. It's a trait shared by many other species—including rhesus monkeys, salamanders, pigeons, raccoons, dolphins, parrots, and dogs. They can compare the exact numbers of a small set of objects at a glance without explicitly counting. This ability is called *subitization,* and it's thought that human babies around six months old also have it. Infant-ologists have shown that babies exposed to images of collections of objects while hearing a number of drumbeats consistently stare longer at the image that matches.

Holt reports that humans have up to three ways of representing numbers, one of which is baked into our biology—subitization. And two more that can be provided by culture—number symbols and number words. Subitization is processed in the part of the brain related to space and time. Numerals are dealt with in the areas of the brain responsible for visual processing and number words in language areas. To go beyond subitization requires a number-labeling system and an understanding of basic algorithms.

This tight connection between numbers and language can be easily demonstrated. For example, multiplication tables seem to be stored as facts in the language parts of the brain. Bilinguals revert to the language of their first arithmetic education when doing multiplication. Another illustration is from our working memory, which we use to remember things like phone numbers. The problem with working memory is that it's a very limited space. And we all know how useful it is to repeatedly say things we are trying to remember (either out loud or to ourselves). Our short-term working memory operates phonologically. English speakers can typically hold seven digits. The Chinese, on the other hand, can typically remember ten digits. Why? Because Chinese digit words are all single syllables—whereas ours are not.[3]

Speaking of what our memories can hold, Stephen Pinker, the leading cognitive linguist, believes that our long-term memory can hold between 50,000 and 100,000 words and, interestingly, "probably at least as many idioms" or other predefined expressions.[4] He also notes a surprising fact about the statistics of words. The more frequently used words tend to have more meanings (they are more polysemic). Pinker puts the number of definitions for the simple, single-syllable word "set" at 80. Set also features in Bill Bryson's *Mother Tongue* in an illustration of the same point. He relates that the *Oxford English Dictionary* takes 60,000 words to define the word set. That's more words than in this entire book!

Computational linguists are using statistics to analyze very large samples of written and spoken language in what are called "corpus studies." Fittingly, for a company whose name embodies large numbers, Google has made freely available a trillion-word corpus of online text. Among the more trivial results of corpus studies are that "the" is the most frequently used word in written English, but "I" is the most frequent word in spoken English. Apparently we are all talking about ourselves a lot.

The *scientifically correct* data show how much we talk about ourselves varies by gender. Michael Gazzaniga reports in his great book *Human* that men and women spend roughly equal amounts of time gossiping.[5] The only exception is that men gossip less when in the presence of women (when other motives are dominant). When men gossip, they spend two-thirds of their time talking about themselves, whereas women only spend one third.[6] Speaking of gender differences, corpus studies show that in written English, the word "he" is the 15th most frequent word, whereas "she" is 30th. Corpus studies have also shown that idioms, despite their inherent inefficiencies, are much more frequently used in spoken English. Something about idioms must be advantageous, or at least popular.

Enough words—let's look at what the numbers are telling us:

For us a *bird in the hand is worth two in the bush,* but to a Spaniard, "a bird in the hand is worth a hundred flying." Chinese are more cautious than we; they "think thrice before acting." For us, *two heads are better than one;* Hindi speakers, however, ask the pertinent question "Who has two heads?", though what they mean is "Who would be so rash as to throw away his life?" Sometimes they can answer the first question: A "two-headed woman" in

Hindi is pregnant. The Chinese prefer one more head; for them, "three heads and six arms" means a superman. And when *push comes to shove,* Hindi speakers get much headier—"having a hundred thousand heads" means being very persistent.

A rash Spaniard would "look for three feet on a cat," meaning he would get involved with something that could be harmful. It could also be harmful to a Spaniard to tell you exactly what he thinks, which would be "to tell the four truths" or, more musically and numerously, to "sing the forty to someone." An ultimately too harmful activity would lead to a Hindi speaker's body "dissolving into the five constituents."

Ever wondered how many cooks will spoil the broth? For the Chinese it's "seven hands and eight legs," which means to do something in a disorganized manner or, similarly, with "seven mouths and eight tongues," meaning everyone talking at the same time. Conversely Japanese "with eight mouths and eight hands" are eloquent and capable on the surface.

Another thought: Does the size of your head matter? For foreheads, it certainly does—an unintelligent Spaniard doesn't have "two fingers' length of forehead," and conversely a super intelligent Russian has "seven inches of forehead." Or how about this one: How many lies are in a pack? For the Japanese, it's "eight hundred lies." And finally, ever wondered how many ordinary men a hero is worth? For a Hindi speaker a hero is "one man worth fifty-two."

ZERO

- A zero on the left: *a person of no account (Arabic)*
- It is better to have no saint than to have six: *too many cooks spoil the broth (Hindi)*

ONE

- Better one living word than a hundred dead ones: *proverb (German)*
- One bird in the dish is better than a hundred in the air: *proverb (German)*
- Catch two pigeons with one fava bean: *kill two birds with one stone (Italian)*
- A bird in the hand is worth a hundred flying: *proverb (Spanish)*
- If you play alone you will win: *proverb (Arabic, Syria)*
- With one rear end you can't sit on two horses: *proverb (Yiddish)*
- One hand cannot hold two water melons: *one thing at a time (Farsi)*
- The one-eyed person is a beauty in the country of the blind: *proverb (Arabic)*
- Never try to use one hand to catch two frogs: *proverb (Chinese)*
- One sheath cannot keep two swords: *proverb (India)*

TWO

- To be two fingers' distance from death: *at death's door (French)*
- To not have two fingers' length of forehead: *to be stupid (Spanish)*
- To be [remain] at two sails: *to not understand (Spanish)*
- To give two answers: *to give enthusiastic consent (Japanese)*
- With two answers: *eagerly, readily (Japanese)*
- To use two tongues: *to tell a lie (Japanese)*
- Two-tongued: *a snake, untrustworthy (Hindi)*

To have one's feet on two boats
Hindi: to fall between two stools

- Father of two tongues: *hypocritical, two-faced person* (*Arabic*)
- Twice born: *a Brahmin, high caste person* (*Hindi*)
- To have one's feet on two boats: *to fall between two stools* (*Hindi*)
- Who has two heads?: *Who would be so rash as to throw away his life?* (*Hindi*)
- You can't dance at two weddings at the same time: *proverb* (*Yiddish*)
- A two-headed woman: *a pregnant woman* (*Sanskrit/Hindi*)
- Two barrels of tears will not heal a bruise: *proverb* (*Chinese*)
- The one who hunts two hares will catch neither: *proverb* (*French*)
- He who seeks revenge should remember to dig two graves: *proverb* (*China*)
- In two kicks: *quickly* (*Spanish, Mexico*)

THREE

- Tall as three apples: *knee-high to a grasshopper, short* (*French*)
- To be the third inconvenience: *third/fifth wheel* (*Italian*)
- To look for three feet on the cat: *to get involved in something harmful* (*Spanish*)
- Neither three nor four: *neither fish nor fowl* (*Chinese*)
- Spittle three feet long: *crave, yearn for* (*Chinese*)

- Think thrice before you act: *look before you leap (Chinese)*
- The good fortune of three lives: *a fortuitous encounter, to be lucky (Chinese)*
- A guest and a fish after three days are poison: *proverb (France)*
- After three days without reading talk becomes flavorless: *proverb (Chinese)*
- A kind word warms for three winters: *proverb (Chinese)*
- When three go together, there is trouble: *proverb (Hindi)*
- Three and five: *squabbling; trickery, machination (Hindi)*
- Seeing the three times: *to be omniscient, see past, present, future (Hindi)*
- Only three things in life are certain—birth, death, and change: *proverb (Arabic)*
- Slander slays three persons–the speaker, the spoken to, and the spoken of: *proverb (Hebrew)*

FOUR

- Four-dollar outfit: *cheap outfit, badly dressed (Italian)*
- Four-coin magazine: *cheap magazine (Italian)*
- To be pulled/drawn by four pins: *dressed to the nines (French)*
- To cut a hair in four: *to split hairs (French)*
- To work like four: *to work like mad, work like a dog (French)*
- The week with four Thursdays: *when hell freezes over, never (French)*

- To tell someone the four truths: *to tell exactly what one thinks (Spanish)*
- To bring four eyes together: *to meet the glance (Hindi)*
- Of four hours: *a short, favorable period (Hindi)*

FIVE

- To send one's five: *to punch (French)*
- The fifth pine: *far away (Spanish)*
- To be in the fifth sleep: *to be fast asleep (Spanish, Mexico)*

Five fires
Hindi: punishment, sitting in the sun in hot weather

- The five supreme gods: *a village court or tribunal* (*Hindi*)
- Five fires: *punishment, sitting in the sun in hot weather* (*Hindi*)
- Dissolution [of the body] into its five constituents: *death* (*Hindi*)

SIX

- All six vital organs failing: *to be stupefied, stunned* (*Chinese*)
- Every sixth six months: *once in a blue moon* (*Hindi*)
- Six doors: *astonished, perplexed* (*Hindi*)
- Where six can eat, seven can eat: *there's always room for one more* (*Spanish*)
- With three heads and six arms: *a superman* (*Chinese*)

SEVEN

- Have seven lives like dogs: *have nine lives* (*Italian*)
- To sweat seven shirts: *to work hard* (*Italian*)
- To be in seventh heaven: *to be on cloud nine* (*Italian and French*)
- Seven mouths and eight tongues: *all talking at the same time* (*Chinese*)
- Seven inches in a forehead: *as wise as Solomon* (*Russian*)

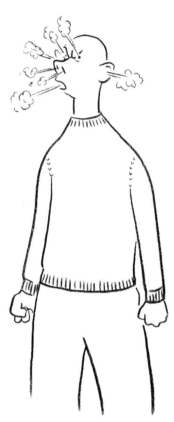

Smoke belches from the seven openings on the head
Chinese: very angry

- Standing there like a seven of spades: *looking stupid*
  (*German*)
- To vilify ancestors to the seventh generation: *to curse
  severely* (*Hindi*)

- Having seven husbands: *a loose woman (Hindi)*
- The seven utterances: *the marriage vows (Hindi)*
- Smoke belches from the seven openings on the head: *very angry (Chinese)*
- Seven trades but no luck: *proverb (Arabic)*
- Seven Fridays in a week: *can't make up your mind (Russian)*

EIGHT

- To become an eight: *to be confused (Spanish, Puerto Rico)*
- To make oneself into an eight: *to complicate one's life (Spanish, Dominican Republic)*
- Eight bushels of talent: *have immense knowledge (Chinese)*
- Eight watches: *24 hours a day (Hindi)*
- Seven hands and eight legs: *too many cooks spoil the broth (Chinese)*
- Eight mouths and with eight hands: *to seem eloquent (Japanese)*
- A beauty to all eight directions: *a sycophant (Japanese)*
- To try whether it's one or eight: *to put in full effort (Japanese)*
- Milk of every eighth day: *a cowherd's payment in kind (Hindi)*

Seven hands and eight legs

Chinese: too many cooks in the kitchen

NINE

- To have the nine treasures: *to have all that the heart desires (Hindi)*
- The nine continents: *the nine fabled regions of the world, all corners (Hindi)*
- Those who have ten miles to go, must regard nine as only halfway: *proverb (German)*
- A single hair from nine oxen: *a drop in the bucket (Hindi)*
- To have the nine treasures and twelve magical powers: *to have all that the heart can desire (Hindi)*

TEN

- The ten directions: *eight points of the compass plus zenith and nadir (Hindi)*
- A smile will gain you ten more years of life: *proverb (China)*
- If bravery is ten, nine is strategy: *proverb (Turkey)*
- Not one of the timid ten: *not a wallflower, not timid (Russian)*
- Ten people–ten different colors: *it takes all sorts (Japanese)*
- Just like ten other people: *average ordinary person (Japanese)*

MANY MANY

- Put oneself in a shirt of eleven rods: *bite off more than one can chew (Spanish)*
- To keep in one's thirteen: *to persist in doing something (Spanish)*
- All sixteen [traditional] adornments: *elaborate make-up [of a woman] (Hindi)*
- The eighteenth: *one's forte (Japanese)*
- Twenty-two misfortunes: *a walking catastrophe (Russian)*
- To put yourself on your thirty-one: *to get all dressed up (French)*
- To see thirty-six candles: *to see stars (French)*
- Of the thirty-six alternatives, running away is the best: *proverb (Chinese)*
- To sing the forty to someone: *to speak unpleasant truth (Spanish)*
- One man worth fifty-two: *a hero (Hindi)*
- Fifty-six knives: *a dangerous woman (Hindi)*
- To put someone to the hundred: *to excite (Spanish)*
- With a hundred lives: *with all one's heart (Hindi)*
- One hundred holes and one thousand wounds: *state of ruin (Chinese)*
- To do the one hundred steps: *to pace the floor, be anxious (French)*
- To strike the four hundred blows: *to run wild, sow one's wild oats (French)*

- Eight hundred lies: *completely untrue, a pack of lies (Japanese)*
- Ten thousand horses charging forward: *to rush headlong, to dive in (Chinese)*
- Ten thousand things rest: *it's finished (Japanese)*
- To have a hundred thousand heads: *to be doggedly persistent (Hindi)*

When the crayfish sings on the mountain

Russian: when hell freezes over, never

chapter eight

TIME

When dogs were tied with sausages

Now for some thoughts on time. Much of the popular literature on anthropological language comparisons tends to be snooty. It has the tone of first worlders looking down their noses (or "looking over their shoulders," as the Germans would say) at "less developed" cultures. Time provides an example where a less developed culture could look down its nose at us. The Kawesqar are a tribe in Chile that have featured frequently in language debates. Charles Darwin encountered them before he wrote *On the Origin of Species,* and he noted that their survival in a cold damp corner of the Patagonia reinforced his belief that mankind is another animal well adapted to its environment.

The Kawesqar have no future tense in their grammar. Their past tense, however, is much more specific, more finely grained, and more evocative than ours. As reported in the *New York Times,* their grammar makes distinctions between "a few seconds ago, a few days ago, a time so long ago that you were not the original observer ... but you know the observer yourself and, finally, a mythological past, a tense the Kawesqar use to suggest that the story is so old that it no longer possesses fresh descriptive truth but rather that other truth which emerges from stories that retain their narrative power despite constant repetition."[1] These people could teach us a *thing or two* about the nature of the past. And about the nature of human memory.

Darwin knew what later scientists now understand neurobiologically, and what our legal system still refuses to acknowledge, that "memory is so deceptive that it ought not to be trusted."[2] That's something we should all know. Even though we might need artists to bring it to our attention. A task done admirably by Jonah Lehrer in *Proust Was a Neuroscientist*, in which he quotes Proust: "It is a labor in vain to try to recapture memory" and "The only paradise is paradise lost." Lehrer elaborates: "Every memory is full of errors"; indeed, the act of remembering changes the memory (a process called *reconsolidation*). He continues: "Memories are not like fiction. They are fiction."[3] We are built to remember relatively little and to creatively fill in the holes so that we seem to have a complete picture.

Another remarkable example of how differently time can be thought of comes from Stephen Pinker's exhilarating book, *The Stuff of Thought*. In it he tells of the Aymara, a people whose metaphor for time is spatially the opposite of ours. Their culture views the past as being physically ahead of them and the future as being physically behind them.[4] The logic is that we can know the past, just as we can know what is in front of us. But the future is not so easily seen, like what's physically behind us.

All languages are constantly changing (even discounting the effects of cultural chafing). John McWhorter, in his excellent book *Word on the Street,* describes how linguists look at this inevitable process. He means not just drift in word meanings (see below) or in the use of metaphors or idioms, but also in more fundamental ways like changes in rules of grammar and syntax. McWhorter's position is that language is just a communication system "that is at all times in the process of becoming a different one." This is more evident in speech than in text, because when writing we edit and consciously revise, rather than just communicate. This sort of change doesn't compromise the fundamental ability to communicate.

One of McWhorter's compelling examples is how the language of Shakespeare, in just 400 years, has become noticeably less understandable. Many readers will know that when Juliet stands upon her balcony, in what the Spanish might call the "pluck the turkey" scene, and pleads, "Wherefore art thou Romeo?", she is asking "Why?", which is what "wherefore" meant. Fewer readers, however, will likely understand the intended meaning in *Love's Labor Lost* of: "with his royal finger thus dally with my excrement." It's not nearly as repulsively scatological or Freudian as it sounds to us today. Back then, excrement could mean any outgrowth, like hair, nails, or feathers. As McWhorter points out, someone fluent in Middle English, as spoken in Chaucer's day, would have to learn modern English as if it were a completely foreign language.

Sol Steinmetz, in his lovely book on etymological drift, *Semantics Antics,* explains why long ago (as the Uruguayans say, "when dogs were tied with sausages") you wouldn't have wanted to be nice, smart, or handsome but would rather have been a bully, or silly, or sad, and why you would have wanted to be insulted but not to have too many hobbies. *Nice* originally meant someone who was foolish, ignorant, senseless, or absurd (middle English 1300). *Smart* for the first 300 years of its use meant causing pain, sharp, cutting, or severe, a sense that survives in the idiom *smart as a whip* but is now used differently in "whip smart." *Handsome* wasn't complimentary. When coined around 1425, it just meant easily handled; it didn't have its current positive connotation until 1590. *Bully* originally meant "darling or sweetheart" and is often found in this sense in Shakespeare. For example, in *Henry V,* "I love the lovely bully" wasn't a confession of masochism. *Silly* in early Middle English meant "happy," "blissful," "blessed," or "fortunate." *Sad* in Olde Englishe meant "full," "satiated," or "satisfied." *Insult* in the 1500s meant the same as *exult,* which is to "boast," "brag," "triumph" in an insolent way. *Exult* still has a related meaning, but *insult* has changed

When dogs were tied with sausages
Spanish (Uruguay): very long ago

substantially. *Hobbies* in 1375 were ponies, or small horses—a sense that survives in the expression "hobby horse";
it's via a contraction of this sense that the present-day
usage meaning "pastime" developed.

Words can also be entirely lost in the mists of time.
They get relegated to larger and less frequently con-
sulted dictionaries,* and finally suffer the ultimate
insult of being delisted. Ammon Shea, in his wonderfully entertaining book *Reading the OED,* notes some

* *Heavy dictionaries are called* donkey killers *in Mexican Spanish.*

excellent dying words that could be beneficially resuscitated.[5] My favorite candidate for revival is *gymnologize*. It means "to dispute naked, like an Indian philosopher." Shea's book is highly recommended. The following are a small sample of its delights:

- Vocabularian: *one who pays too much attention to words*
- Unlove: *to cease to love a person*
- Tardiloquent: *talking slowly*
- Somnificator: *one who induces sleep in others*
- Sarcast: *a writer or speaker who is sarcastic**
- Natiform: *buttock-shaped*
- Mythistory: *a mythologized account of history*
- Mislove: *to hate, to love in a sinful manner*
- Lant: *to add urine to ale to make it stronger*
- Kakistocracy: *government by the worst citizens*
- Idiorepulsive: *self-repellent*
- Gulchin: *a little glutton!*
- Finifugal: *shunning the end of anything*
- Eumorphous: *well formed*
- Debag: *to strip the pants from a person; punishment or joke*
- Bowelless: *lacking mercy*
- Bedinner: *to treat to dinner*
- Anonymuncle: *an anonymous, small-time writer*

I've previously used the thought image of idioms being frozen metaphors. The occurrence of words no longer in use except in certain idioms is a wonderful flea

---

* *Sarcasm is from the ancient Greek for* flesh-cutting.

in the amber demonstration of this fossilization. For example, we no longer say *kith, shrift, haw, raring, kilter, fangled, fro, spick, boggle,* and *hither,* though we still say "kith and kin," "short shrift," "hem and haw," "raring to go," "off-kilter," "newfangled," "to and fro," "spic and span," "mind-boggling," and "come hither." And while we still say *hue, fell,* and *neck,* their petrified* meanings in "hue and cry," "one fell swoop," and "neck of the woods" aren't what they seem. *Hue* in this usage has nothing to do with color—it's from the Latin for a horn; the expression literally means "horn and shouting." *Fell* meant something terrible—evil, or deadly ferocity (our word felon comes from the same root). *Neck* used to mean a parcel of land.

Okay, enough *bush beating*. Let's spend some time looking at the use of time in idioms (before their meanings change).

Ever wondered how frequent *once in a blue moon* is? For a Yiddish speaker it's "a year and a Wednesday." To a Hindi speaker it's three years; their equivalent expression is "every six six months." To an Italian the concept is less precise, but the interval seems much longer: "every death of a pope." Colombians are less concerned with the rank of the deceased: "each time a bishop dies." For Americans a *month of Sundays* indicates a very long time. For a Frenchman, "the week with four Thursdays" or "every 36th of the month" is *when hell freezes over.* And for a Spaniard Friday the 13th is nothing to worry about; they fear the unlucky Sunday the 7th.

---

* Petrified *shares the same root as* Peter. Petra *in ancient Greek meant "rock."*

QUICK/FAST/YOUNG

- Like a poor person's funeral: *quickly (Spanish, Costa Rica)*
- A white colt passing over a crevice: *time flies, life is short (Chinese)*
- Urgent, like eyebrows on fire: *critical, extremely urgent (Chinese)*
- Are you standing on one leg?: *Are you in a hurry? (Yiddish)*
- With a monkey's tooth: *extremely fast (German)*
- Has eaten little kasha: *is inexperienced (Russian)*

SLOW/LATE

- He creeps like a bedbug: *as slow as molasses (Yiddish)*
- To do the leek: *to hang around waiting (French)*
- To be slow as hunger: *to be as slow as molasses (Italian)*
- Angel is passing by: *pause in the conversation (French)*
- To come late to a place: *to get nervous (Japanese)*

LONG/OLD/PAST

- The days of cherries: *the good old days (French)*
- To smoke once every death of a pope: *once in a blue moon, rarely (Italian)*

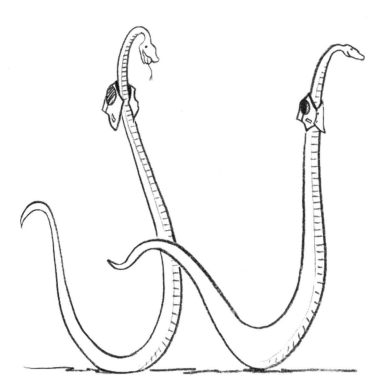

When snakes wore vests
Spanish: very long ago

- Each time a bishop dies: *once in a blue moon, rarely* (*Spanish, Colombia*)
- Older than pinol [toasted corn drink]: *as old as the hills* (*Spanish, Nicaragua*)
- To be for light soup and good wine: *to be old* (*Spanish*)

Time
151

- When snakes wore vests: *a long time ago* (*Spanish, Chile*)
- When dogs were tied with sausages: *very long ago* (*Spanish, Uruguay*)
- In the year of the pear: *a long time ago* (*Spanish*)
- Day when the firemen get paid: *when hell freezes over, never* (*Spanish, Chile*)
- To be ancient lavender: *to be old hat* (*German*)
- Every sixth six months: *once in a blue moon* (*Hindi*)
- A year and a Wednesday: *it will take a long, long time* (*Yiddish*)
- Every 36th of the month: *once in a blue moon, rarely* (*French*)
- When frogs grow hair: *never* (*Spanish, Latin America*)

When frogs grow hair
Spanish (Latin America): never

- Until the seas dry up and the rocks crumble: *forever (Chinese)*
- From birth to birth: *forever (Hindi)*
- When the crayfish sings on the mountain: *when hell freezes over, never (Russian)*

CLOCK

- In all sir God's earliness: *at the crack of dawn (German)*
- To have the midday devil: *midlife crisis (French)*
- The sun is as high as three poles: *about 9 a.m. (Chinese)*
- Praise day before evening: *don't count your chickens before they're hatched (German)*
- Five minutes to twelve: *the eleventh hour, the last minute (German)*

CALENDAR

- Warmed soup: *old hat, yesterday's news (Italian)*
- A daughter of yesterday: *something unexpected and not welcome (Arabic)*
- Don't look for yesterday's fish in a house of the otter: *proverb (Hindi)*
- To have Aprils: *to have a certain age (Spanish)*
- To turn out with her Sunday the 7th: *to have bad luck (Spanish, Costa Rica)*

- To make one's August: *to make hay while the sun shines* (*Spanish*)
- Seven Fridays in one week: *keep changing one's mind* (*Russian*)
- October's cold penetrates the intestines: *proverb* (*Arabic*)
- Look like September: *have a long face, look sad* (*Russian*)
- The month of passion: *February* (*Hindi*)
- The six seasons of the year: (*Hindi*)
- In July the water boils in the water skin [container made of skin]: *proverb* (*Arabic*)

TIME – GENERAL

- To give time: *to fire someone* (*Japanese*)
- To steal time: *to make good use of one's free time* (*Japanese*)
- Each vegetable has its own time: *every dog has its day* (*Russian*)
- To have no time to die: *to be overwhelmed with work* (*Hindi*)
- If you want one year of prosperity, grow grain; if ten years, grow trees; if a hundred years, grow people: *proverb* (*Chinese*)
- One generation plants the tree, another gets the shade: *proverb* (*China*)

- Thought expeller: *pastime, distraction (Italian)*
- The best time to plant a tree is twenty years ago, the second best time is now: *proverb (China)*
- What greater crime than loss of time: *proverb (German)*
- Time is anger's medicine: *time heals all wounds (German)*
- A day of sorrow is longer than a month of joy: *proverb (China)*
- The most wasted of days is one with no laughter: *proverb (French)*
- Gossip lasts seventy-five days: *proverb (Japanese)*
- Rhubarb and patience work wonders: *proverb (German)*
- A dark year: *a curse on you (Yiddish)*
- Seas change into mulberry fields: *time brings great changes (Chinese)*
- Time heals old pains, while it creates new ones: *proverb (Hebrew)*

White clouds change into gray dogs
Chinese: human affairs are unpredictable

chapter nine

COLORS

Sighing with blue breath

W E'VE SEEN HOW DIFFERENTLY different cultures can see the world. But surely since we all have the same visual equipment, we all see something as basic as color in the same way? Wrong. … It turns out that color vision isn't a black-and-white issue. It's not nearly that simple. Language has a significant effect on how we "see" colors—more precisely, on how we divide up and label different parts of the visible spectrum. Our eyes register roughly the same range of light (between the aptly named infra-red and ultra-violet). However, the number of differently labeled segments we use varies. Some languages only distinguish between two basic colors, *black and white* (dark and light). Others add extra colors, typically in the following sequence: red, green, yellow, blue, and brown.[1] This sort of different color categorization is nicely illustrated by the word "grue." Psycholinguists use it to describe languages that make no distinction between blue and green (e.g., Welsh Gaelic).

Apparently, English is unusual in making this distinction; most other languages are grue languages.* Before English speakers swell too much with pride (or, as the Japanese might say, "flap their nose wings"), there are other languages that have single word labels for finer color gradations. Russians have no single word for what we call blue but have different basic color words for light blue (*goluboy*) and dark blue (*siniy*). And that makes Russians faster at distinguishing their blues, their goluboy from their siniy.[2]

It's not only language that affects the way you "see" color. So does your age. Researchers have shown that adults filter color perception through the prism of their language, whereas infants don't. This has been tested on babies as young as four months old. Infant-ologists do this by flashing targets of the same and different color categories in the right and left visual fields of subjects. They measure how quickly eye movements are initiated. It turns out that the speed at which we discriminate color categories is lateralized. Adults are faster with targets in the right visual field (processed by the brain's left hemisphere). Infants, *on the other hand,* are faster in the left visual field. From this finding, researchers have concluded that, as we get older, an unfiltered perception of color gives way to one that is mediated by language. The difference in adults is caused by the influence of lexical color codes in the left hemisphere.[3]

One of the functions of idioms is to make our

---

* Most of the world's 6,000 or so languages are spoken by fewer than a couple of thousand people.

language more colorful, more interesting. We saw in Chapter 5 how incongruity, the "Shakespeared Brain" mechanism, can add color to a turn of phrase. Humor can serve a similar function, of adding color and interest. As Jim Holt points out in his hilarious history *Stop Me If You've Heard This,* many jokes depend on the juxtaposition of *strange bedfellows*.[4] A punchline's dramatic resolution of conflicting elements and the resulting sudden shift of meaning reconciles strange head-fellows.

My favorite of Holt's examples is the old Jewish joke: "Have you taken a bath?" "What. Is there one missing?" Holt notes that Jewish humor is particularly language oriented. A couple of particularly charming examples are from Groucho Marx: to a hostess, "I've had a perfectly wonderful evening. But this wasn't it," and "One morning I shot an elephant in my pajamas. How he got in my pajamas, I'll never know." Idioms must operate somewhat similarly—they also need a sudden shift in meaning. Though, of course, they suffer from too much *old-chestnut*-iness, to cause the mental fireworks set off by a good semantically twisty joke. The shift in a good joke must happen consciously, but idioms are resolved non-consciously.

Speaking of twisty semantics, let's take a look at how colors are used in idioms. As already noted, all languages make the distinction between black and white (dark and light). The Chinese and the Russians both have relevant Orwellian expressions. The Chinese say to "make no difference between black and white," which means to do something indiscriminately. And the Russians say "to take black for white," meaning to be easily fooled.

It's ironic that George Orwell's name has come to signify the worst abuses of language that power can perpetrate. As Clive James notes in his excellent review of Orwell's writings,[5] the same fate has also befallen Franz Kafka. Both their names are now used to describe something they decried and stood against.* James also notes that Orwell, in his journalism during World War II, usually got his guesses about the truth correct by working back from the lies people on the other side were telling.

In his insightful guide *Why Orwell Matters,* Christopher Hitchens points out, "It's likely Orwell would have been appalled by the rise of *political correctness.*[6] Even in its mildest forms, it can be an insidious self-thought-policing. And he would no doubt *turn in his grave* at the ever increasingly doublethinking, doublespeaking, and doubledoing exploits of today's politicians.

Orwell also wrote damningly on idioms, and on the overuse of pre-fabricated figures of speech and canned thoughts. In his essay "Politics and the English Language," he rails against "staleness of imagery," "worn-out metaphors," "accumulation of stale phrases," and the "invasion of one's mind by ready-made phrases."[7] Orwell's prescription for curing this includes as its first rule the admonishment to "never use a metaphor, simile or other figure of speech which you are used to seeing in print." Though he doesn't mention idioms specifically in that list, he does

* *Contra-eponymy?*

include them in an earlier enumeration of suspects. "By using stale metaphors, similes and idioms, you save much mental effort." Here he also indicates his understanding of the enduring value and popularity of idioms and stock phrases. He is correct that such a saving is *penny wise and pound foolish* when trying to write well. We expect our writers to have exerted themselves intellectually, to not have spared any mental effort. That's one of the things that makes it worth our while reading them. However, such *penny wisdom* can be very useful when speaking. Usually we are mainly interested in getting our point across, and idioms and stock phrases, with their economy of mental effort, can do that quite effectively. Particularly when, for some reason, we don't want to do it entirely literally.

SPEAKING OF BLACK

- To grind the black: *to be depressed (French)*
- Black-bellied: *wicked or deceitful (Japanese)*
- Drive black: *ride for free (German)*
- Place a black pot on the head: *bring disgrace on (Hindi)*
- Makes my wedding day black: *causes trouble (Yiddish)*
- Black one: *term of endearment, sweetheart (Spanish)*
- Black butter eye: *bruise, black eye (French)*
- Black-eyed: *unkind, cruel (Hindi)*
- To make eyes black and white: *to roll one's eyes in bewilderment (Japanese)*

- A black cat ran between them: *at an impasse (Russian)*
- A black bee: *A woman's female friend (Hindi)*
- Something black in the lentils: *suspicious (Hindi)*

WHITE

- Make your day white: *have a good day (Arabic)*
- Whitened our faces: *did us great credit (Arabic)*
- White bone: *high born (Italian)*
- White island: *an imaginary home of the blessed (Hindi)*
- The blood to turn white: *to be indifferent (Hindi)*
- Have a white face mask: *look bad due to worry (Spanish)*
- To make an occasion white: *to spoil it (Italian)*
- White night: *sleepless night (Italian)*
- White soot: *an awful mess (Russian)*
- To look with white eyes: *to show disdain (Japanese)*
- White like a nun's butt cheek: *pale (Spanish)*
- Till the white flies: *till the snow falls (Russian)*
- White beak: *inexperienced (French)*
- To see a white mouse: *to see something rare (German)*

RED

- Red movie: *adult entertainment, blue movie (Italian)*
- Red joke: *a rude or off-color joke (Spanish)*
- Deep red lie: *worst kind of lie (Japanese)*

- A red light comes on: *become precarious (Japanese)*
- To stand on the red list: *to be endangered (German)*
- One red spot: *only woman among men (Japanese)*
- The height of a red face: *ashamed of oneself (Japanese)*
- Red coal: *one flushed with anger (Hindi)*
- Red toga: *magistrate (Italian)*
- The red-haired one: *red wine with more body (French)*
- To see everything pink: *to look through rose-colored glasses (French)*
- Today red, tomorrow dead: *here today, gone tomorrow (German)*
- Burn in a poppy* color: *blush (Russian)*
- Paint it pink: *decorate, gild the lily (Spanish)*

GREEN

- Green years: *the best of times (Italian)*
- Be in/at the green: *poor (Italian)*
- Leave as God painted the parakeet: *make someone mad (Spanish, Nicaragua)*
- Green joke, movie, woman, widow, man, or tail: *off-color or dirty (Spanish)*
- Wearing a green hat: *having an unfaithful wife (Chinese)*
- To have a green hand: *to have a green thumb (French)*
- A green number: *a toll-free number (Italian)*
- The last of the green beans: *it's all over (French)*

* *Completely tangential:* Poppycock *derives from the Dutch for doll's poop.*

- Cabbage green and green cabbage: *six of one, a half dozen of the other (French)*
- The green goddess: *marijuana (Spanish)*
- Because of pure green peas: *for no reason (Spanish, Peru)*
- Green sky!: *an expression of surprise (Spanish, Puerto Rico)*

YELLOW

- Yellow: *with envy (German)*
- Yellow colored: *bashful (Hindi)*
- Yellow book: *detective novel (Italian)*
- To smile yellow: *sickly smile (French)*
- Yellow beak: *inexperienced, a greenhorn (Japanese)*
- To see yellow: *the glass is half empty (French)*

BLUE

- See nothing but blue: *be in the dark (French)*
- Blue fury: *in a rage, seeing red (French)*
- Blue prince: *a wonderful man (Spanish)*
- Sighing with blue breath: *suffering (Japanese)*
- To show blue veins: *to be enraged (Japanese)*
- To be blue: *to be plastered (Russian)*
- To lie the blue out of the sky: *to be completely dishonest (German)*

- To make blue: *to take the day off* (*German*)
- Blue eye: *black eye, bruise on face* (*German*)
- Blue hour: *time before dusk, especially in winter* (*German*)
- To have blue nails: *to be near death* (*Hindi*)
- To rise sharply like blue clouds: *meteoric rise* (*Chinese*)
- To experience a blue wonder: *to get a nasty surprise* (*German*)
- Blue haze: *rubbish* (*German*)

COLOR IN GENERAL

- Change one's eye color: *a serious look* (*Japanese*)
- A trick of color: *a pretense of love* (*Japanese*)
- To turn color: *to turn red with anger* (*Japanese*)
- Paint yourself [in color]: *to go away* (*Spanish, Mexico*)
- Laugh at colored fish: *not worry* (*Spanish, Cuba*)
- To observe the color of the banner: *to sit on the fence* (*Japanese*)
- To show a difficult color: *to express disapproval* (*Japanese*)
- Under the one color: *birds of a feather* (*Russian*)
- Known like a colorful dog: *to be a well-known figure* (*German*)
- To change color like a chameleon: *to flush or turn pale [with anger]* (*Hindi*)
- At night all cats are dark-colored: *proverb* (*Spanish*)

Stop climbing on my head
Arabic: stop annoying me

chapter ten

EMOTIONAL STATES

Bang your butt on the ground

S ADNESS AND HAPPINESS are emotional states. So are Spain and Italy. Some expressions vividly illustrate differences between cultures. But all cultures also share some. I'm not talking about verbal expressions; I mean facial expressions. As we say in English, what we are feeling is often *written all over our faces,* while Russians are more specific; for them "it is written on the forehead." Yiddish and Hindi have similar expressions, though in both these cases it's not your feelings, it's your fate, that's on display.

Facial expressions are a key way in which we send information about our emotional states. Though we don't think of them in quite this way now, Charles Darwin included facial expressions in his definition of language. And he didn't limit the ability to read them consistently to just humans. He wrote a whole book to record his feelings on the subject, *The Expression of the Emotions in Man and Animal,** in which he says, "The

---

* *Darwin also wrote lesser known books on barnacles, orchids, shipboard microscopy, the movements of climbing plants, insectivorous plants, vegetable mold, and worms, none of which I've read.*

young and the old of widely different races, both with man and animals, express the same state of mind by the same movements." Idioms capture some of the universality of this connection between faces and feelings. For example, when a Puerto Rican says that someone had "a face like a busy telephone," it's not hard to guess that she means that person was angry.

Our ability to non-consciously and rapidly identify other people's emotional state from their facial expressions can wonderfully be thought of as a form of mind reading. Another way to think of it is that our faces are neuro-transmitters. This sort of neuro-transmitting is one of our earliest pre-linguistic forms of communication. By earliest I mean not just in terms of ancient history. We all still do this pre-linguistic mind-sharing today. As babies we communicate this way. And as Darwin indicated, all of us use a core set of basic facial expressions that convey universal meaning. These have been exhaustively (and painfully*) catalogued by Paul Ekman and his colleagues at the University of California at San Francisco (UCSF). They developed the Facial Action Coding System (FACS). Some of this newly rediscovered facial wisdom can also be found in the timeless wisdom of idioms—for example, the Japanese idiom "one's cheek gets loose" means to smile, and "to make one's eyes triangular" means to look angrily at someone.

FACS[1] breaks all possible facial expressions into 40 or

---

* *They had their own facial muscles electrically stimulated by surgeons in the process of creating the catalogue over a period of seven years.*

so "action units," each of which corresponds to the tightening or relaxation of particular muscles (my favorite is called the "nostril dilator"—which Japanese pay attention to in their idiom "to move the wings of one's nose incessantly," meaning to brag or to have a swelled head). The thousands of possible combinations of facial contortions can be *boiled down* into seven categories that are shared by all of us—happiness, sadness,* anger, disgust, neutral, fear, and surprise. There is less certainty about the reliable interpretation of indicators of other emotions like shame and contempt. However, the core set are thought to be innate—though they've never seen them, people blind from birth still use them. As well as being innate, the core set is at least to some degree involuntary. When you feel one of those emotions, you can't help but move the relevant facial muscles to the appropriate configuration. It seems we are built to automatically advertise certain emotional states to those around us. We are built to be emotionally "leaky," to automatically and prelinguistically share our state of mind.

The adaptive benefits of this emotional leaking have been shown. We are particularly attuned to quickly noticing fearful faces, which we do faster than the 40 milliseconds it takes us to notice happy or neutral ones. We quickly and non-consciously sort out whether someone looks fearful and bring the implied potential threat to the attention of our conscious minds. The

* *The French have a word for a "grief muscle" that Darwin mentions in another essay on expressions.*

effect works with just images of eyes. It seems that in addition to being emotionally leaky, we are built to be emotionally contagious.

The origins and development of human language (language origin-ology) are still an area of heated debate among the relevant experts. Some linguists get very emotional about it. They believe that language emerged from our undeniable urge to expletively express exasperation and other extreme emotions: to "eff" the ineffable. Cursing may have been the precursor of all language, polite or otherwise. Ironically for those skilled in the use of, rather than the study of, language, this view has come to be known as the "poo-poo" theory. Steven Pinker, one of our foremost psycholinguists, subscribes to this view. He politely expresses it thus: "Since swearing involves clearly more ancient parts of the brain, it could be a missing link between animal vocalization and human language."[2] In his torrent-of-thought-provoking *The Stuff of Thought,* Pinker also notes that brain-damage-ology has been helpful. Sufferers from some brain injuries can have difficulty with language, while their ability to *swear like sailors* can be left entirely intact. That establishes a neuro-anatomical connection between curses and idioms. Pinker says the "survival of swearing in aphasia suggests that taboo epithets are stored prefabricated in the right hemisphere ... [which] also can sometimes store idiosyncratic [language elements]"[3] (most of our language processing is done by our left brains).

While some idioms highlight cultural differences and some illustrate similarities, others are just plain bizarre. For example, when English speakers might *die laughing,* a similarly amused Frenchman would "bang his butt on the ground" and an equally tickled Japanese would be at least as uncomfortable in having his "stomach skin distorted" or, worse, might get her "jaw dislocated." More astoundingly, an equivalently entertained Japanese might "make tea with his navel." There will be more on talented navel maneuvers in following chapters.

Speaking of bizarre, though we all share a core set of facial expressions—it seems some folks have particularly talented faces. When an English speaker might *fly off the handle,* a similarly aggravated Chinese might display an astonishing ability to "belch smoke from the seven orifices of the head."

Let's see what else expressions that demonstrate emotions or states of mind reveal about the minds of people from other states:

Making tea with your navel
Japanese: laughable

HAPPY/CONTENT

- A face full of spring air: *radiant with happiness (Chinese)*
- With dancing eyebrows and a radiant face: *enraptured (Chinese)*
- To be happy as castanets: *ecstatic (Spanish)*
- To hang heaven full of violins: *to be ecstatic (German)*
- Live like a maggot in bacon: *be very happy (German)*
- To fart in silk: *to be very happy (French)*
- As happy as a fiancé: *highest happiness (Russian)*
- Lamps to burn with ghee/butter: *living in high style (Hindi)*
- The end is musk: *a happy ending (Arabic)*
- To feel poodle-well: *to be on top of the world, ecstatic (German)*
- To lower the outside corners of one's eyes: *to be pleased (Japanese)*

SMILING/LAUGHING

- To peel the teeth: *to smile (Spanish, Mexico)*
- Peeled as a banana: *dying of laughter (Spanish, Puerto Rico)*
- Bang your butt on the ground: *die laughing (French)*
- Makes the chickens laugh: *hilarious (Russian)*
- To distort one's stomach skin: *to die laughing (Japanese)*

- To loosen one's cheek: *to smile (Japanese)*
- Making tea with your navel: *being laughable (Japanese)*
- To embrace one's own belly: *to laugh one's head off (Japanese)*
- To dislocate one's jaw: *to die laughing (Japanese)*
- One side painful: *laugh so hard it hurts (Japanese)*
- Lizard's laughter: *false or forced laughter (Yiddish)*

SAD/UNHAPPY/SULKY

- To have the cockroach: *to have the blues (French)*
- To have tears in your pocket: *to be easily moved to tears (Italian)*
- To have fallen ears: *to be crestfallen (Spanish)*
- To look like September: *to have a long face (Russian)*
- A stepmother's face: *a sullen look (Chinese)*
- To play the insulted liver sausage: *to sulk (German)*
- Stand like a watered poodle: *crestfallen (German)*
- To loosen the turban: *to be crestfallen (Hindi)*
- Addressing the ground: *dejected (Hindi)*
- To twist one's navel: *to sulk (Japanese)*
- The front of one's eyes gets dark: *feel depressed (Japanese)*
- Vomit the sound of weakness: *whine (Japanese)*
- To walk with a suitcase: *to be in a bad mood (Spanish, Chile)*
- With a cloudy face: *sad (Japanese)*
- The heart to burn: *to grieve/mourn (Hindi)*

With a cloudy face
Japanese: sad

- To lower the ears: *to give in (Spanish)*
- To be covered in mud: *to be defeated (Japanese)*
- A day of sorrow is longer than a month of joy:
  proverb (China)

IRRITATED/ANNOYED/UPSET

- To make music: *to complain (French)*
- To make a slice of bread and butter: *to make a fuss (French)*
- Let the dolls dance: *complain (German)*
- Big ugly bedbug: *a person who gets angry easily (Spanish, Argentina)*
- Like a little match: *quick-tempered (Spanish, Puerto Rico)*
- Stop climbing on my head: *stop annoying me (Arabic)*
- To have the face of bad milk: *to be in a bad mood (Spanish)*
- To have a lemon face: *look annoyed (Spanish, Mexico)*
- To have a face like a busy telephone: *to be annoyed (Spanish, Puerto Rico)*
- To look for someone's fleas: *to provoke or irritate (Spanish, Mexico)*
- Don't twist my head: *don't annoy me (Yiddish)*
- To pierce the eye: *to irritate (Hindi)*
- To not be a pear in sugar: *to be disagreeable (Spanish, Mexico)*
- To have bad grape: *to have a gruff or severe demeanor (Spanish)*
- A lot of Christmases with no Christmas Eve: *a bitter person (Spanish, Puerto Rico)*
- To bend the spiral of hair on the crown of one's head: *to be nasty (Japanese)*
- One's belly balloons: *to get frustrated [from keeping quiet] (Japanese)*

- Where the mountains and rivers end: *at the end of one's rope, at wit's end* (*Chinese*)
- To be wool gathering: *to be at wit's end* (*Hindi*)
- To step on a favorite corn: *to hit a nerve* (*Russian*)

ANGRY

- To leave someone the way God painted the parakeet: *to make someone mad* (*Spanish, Nicaragua*)
- To lose the stirrup: *to lose one's temper* (*Italian and Spanish*)
- Anger hair points to heaven: *livid, hopping mad* (*Japanese*)
- To have one's liver twist: *to get angry* (*Spanish, Mexico*)
- To have the mustard rise up: *to get angry* (*Spanish, Peru*)
- Dandruff attack: *fit, tantrum* (*Spanish, South America*)
- Smoke belches from the seven openings on the head: *fuming angry* (*Chinese*)
- To make one's eyes triangular: *to look angrily at someone* (*Japanese*)
- One's belly boils over: *to be furious* (*Japanese*)
- To climb up the coconut tree: *to fly off the handle* (*French*)
- To get horns like an animal: *to get very upset or angry* (*Spanish, Nicaragua*)
- To anger one green and blue: *to be so angry as to see red* (*German*)
- To show blue veins: *to become enraged* (*Japanese*)
- Led to a white knee: *roused to fury* (*Russian*)

A fly on the nose
Italian: a chip on the shoulder

- To roll on glowing coals: *to burn with rage, envy (Hindi)*
- Standing on someone's eyebrows: *very angry (Spanish)*
- Gotten in the wool: *had a fight (German)*
- To send one's five: *to punch (French)*
- To damage someone's portrait: *to bash someone's face (French)*
- To give someone a big head: *to bash someone's face (French)*

- To de-testicle: *to ruin, to mess up (Spanish, Mexico)*
- To purée: *to beat someone up (Spanish, Mexico)*
- To leave with a flick of one's sleeve: *to leave upset (Chinese)*
- Time is anger's medicine: *time heals (German)*

CRAZY/MAD

- To have one on the waffle: *to be crazy (German)*
- To have a hunting license: *to be a certified lunatic (German)*
- To wrestle alone: *to tilt at windmills (Japanese)*
- To have mambo in the head: *to be confused (Spanish, Argentina)*
- Not knowing which foot to dance on: *confused (French)*
- The roof has slid off: *to become crazy (Russian)*
- To have a spider on the ceiling: *to be crazy (French)*
- To be gotten out of the little house: *to be wild, excited (German)*
- To have a hammer: *to be around the bend (German)*

SURPRISED/ASTONISHED*

- To be left with the square face: *to be very surprised (Spanish, Mexico)*
- Enough to cure hiccups: *astonishing (Spanish, Latin America)*

---

*Astonishment *originally meant "to be struck by lightning."*

- To smash one's liver: *to be flabbergasted, amazed (Japanese)*
- To straighten one's collar: *to be awestruck (Japanese)*
- Bite the finger between the teeth: *to be utterly astonished (Hindi)*

OTHER ASSORTED EMOTIONAL EXPRESSIONS OR EXPRESSIONS OF STATES OF MIND

- To have a soap: *to be afraid (Spanish, Argentina)*
- Shiver though not cold: *tremble with fear (Chinese)*
- Have one's testicles to zero: *be very frightened (French)*
- Like a crocodile in a wallet factory: *very nervous (Spanish, Puerto Rico)*
- Like a dog in a canoe: *very nervous (Spanish, Puerto Rico)*
- One's legs don't touch the ground: *restless, excited (Japanese)*
- The lips are dry: *to be nervous (Hindi)*
- Spittle three feet long: *to crave, yearn (Chinese)*
- To put a finger in one's mouth: *look enviously (Japanese)*
- Throw flowers at yourself: *be boastful (Spanish, Latin America)*
- To kiss the sky: *to show great conceit (Hindi)*
- To think one is the last suck on the mango: *to think one is hot stuff (Spanish, South America)*

To flap the wings of one's nose incessantly
Japanese: to swell with pride

- To think one is the navel of the world:* *to think too highly of oneself (Spanish)*
- To think one is the hole in the center of the cake: *to think too highly of oneself (Spanish, Chile)*
- To flap the wings of one's nose incessantly: *to swell with pride (Japanese)*
- To have a face that is noseless: *to be without shame (Hindi)*
- Cat scratches on the soul: *something gnawing at one's heart (Russian)*
- To have thick face skin: *to be shameless (Japanese)*
- To drink a mouthful of blood: *to have a bitter or humiliating experience (Hindi)*
- To break the heart's blisters: *to relieve the suffering of heart or mind (Hindi)*
- A fly on the nose: *a chip on the shoulder (Italian)*

* *In ancient Rome, a returning victorious general was given a triumph, a lavish parade in his honor—at which a slave was employed to constantly remind the general that he was still only human.*

To shoot at sparrows with a cannon
German: to overkill, to overdo

chapter eleven

WORK & MONEY

To have no time to die

INCREASINGLY WORK CAUSES "time-poverty." That's an alarming thought, ending in an alarming expression. It's not an idiom. Its intended meaning is quite clear. It connects work to the most essential fact of life—that time is limited. Too often we decide to minimize our money-poverty at the expense of our time-richness.

Time-poverty is on the rise everywhere and is at epidemic proportions in the United States. Debra Satz, an associate professor at Stanford, puts it thus: "Medieval peasants worked less than you."[1] The "you" in this case being the American worker. That's astonishing (or, in Mexican Spanish, "enough to cure hiccups"). Philosophers, economists, psychologists, futurologists, oracles, and seers of all kinds all assumed that as we got richer and as technology and gadgets reduced the amount of time and effort required to get things done, we would choose to have more leisure. Turns out they were all precisely wrong. And I still don't have my flying car. Recent research has shown that in the U.S. the well-off have less leisure time than the less well off. That's a perversion of human nature. The insatiable drives of modern capitalism and *keeping up with the Joneses* (nowadays, keeping ahead of the Chois and the Kumars) have pushed Americans to this unnatural state of affairs. I say unnatural because all stable systems in nature have balancing forces that impose limits. That's one of the inherent instabilities in modern capitalism. It unnaturally resists limits. Its ruthless focus on short-term maximization at the expense of all else leads to many ills. It just keeps going till its input resources are exhausted.* And let's not forget that the workers themselves are one of those resources. As the revealing expression has it, you are a human resource; you are a not-always-necessary and fungible input to the profit machine. It's designed to keep going until you and all its other inputs are exhausted. Modern capitalism just doesn't have enough enough-ness in it. And so, sadly, neither do our lives.

Having overworked that thought, let's see how overworked Americans are. On average, workers in the U.S. toil about 350 hours per year more than Europeans. Let's do the math (or, as we would more prolifically say in England, the maths). Assuming 8-hour days (which I know is a little unrealistic), that's more than 40 working days or 8 work weeks! While the fact that Americans work longer is well known (and even bragged about by some politicians

---

* Some would retort that competition imposes limits. Well, sort of, but not in a useful sense. Competitors out-consume each other in relation to resources until there aren't any more inputs left to compete with.

and time-poor business types), what is less well known is that average productivity per hour in France is higher. And the French take the whole of August off every year! Speaking of vacation, more than a hundred other countries have mandatory minimum paid-leave laws. Europeans have between four and five weeks*; the Japanese two weeks. The U.S. has zero, and on average only one in seven workers gets more than two weeks vacation. ...

Okay, that's enough of a break ... I feel like I need to get back to work. ...

Back to my rant against the excesses of modern capitalism—and it is the unlimited excess of the modern variety that I find objectionable. I'd like to revive a connection between humanity's essential nature (her leaky, contagious emotions, her morality, and the proper role for his rationality) and the visible handiwork of one of capitalism's founders, Adam Smith. Smith has suffered the fate of many founders. If he found out what we were up to with his legacy, he would be dismal indeed. *The Wealth of Nations* is now thought of as the intellectual wellspring of laissez-faire** economic policies, which in turn is a cornerstone of modern capitalism. I'd argue his legacy has been misrepresented—perhaps beyond recognition—meaning it's time for a re-cognition, for serious rethinking.

---

* *For some Europeans even this is meager; Romans in A.D. 354 had 177 festival days.*

** *The term* laissez-faire *is invisible in Smith's writings. He believed government had a necessary role.*

I know all this only by virtue of having read secondary sources. The primary ones are just too tome-ly (900-plus pages and 500-plus pages). In these times of increasing time-poverty, timeless wisdoms must be accessible in less time. Wisdom is of no use if it's entomb-ed in books so long that no one has time any longer to read them. Authors need to pay attention, on our behalf, to our attention deficits. Keep it short and sweet. Straying from that thought, I'm reminded of a quotation from one famously voluminous author to another: Henry James said of Marcel Proust's style that it was "an inconceivable boredom associated with the most extreme ecstasy which it is possible to imagine."[2] These days, let's keep it to just the ecstasy, please.

I've once again relied on those more talented and dedicated to do the hard work and to summarize (and, I hope, not to lie to me): firstly, *On The Wealth of Nations* (256 pages) by P. J. O'Rourke, that witty and cultured commentator and notorious communist sympathizer; secondly, on *The Authentic Adam Smith* (144 pages) by James Buchan, a former foreign correspondent for that stridently anti-capitalist rag, the *Financial Times* of London. Each concludes that there was much more to Smith than the *cherry-picked* legacy of *The Wealth of Nations*. Both agree that Smith gave primacy to moral matters. Smith's first tome was called *The Theory of Moral Sentiments*.

Allow me to illustrate with my favorite cherries from these secondary sources. Comrade O'Rourke says, "It is a mistake to read *The Wealth of Nations* as a justification of amoral greed"[3] and "avarice and injustice are always short sighted."[4] Buchan declares his aims: to "restore to Smith's biography the primacy of feeling over reason" and to "show that *The Theory of Moral Sentiments* ... is good economics."[5] He also points out that *Moral Sentiments* was more economically successful. It outsold *Wealth of Nations* until the Victorian era (when industrialists perhaps needed more justification for their extreme practices). Buchan quotes *Moral Sentiments'* opening line from the first chapter, "On the Propriety of Action": "How selfish soever man may be supposed, there are evidently some principles in his nature, which interest him in the fortune of others, and render their happiness necessary to him, though he derives nothing from it except the pleasure of seeing it."[6] That paragraph ends with the further observation that "for this sentiment ... is by no means confined to the virtuous and humane. ... The greatest ruffian, the most hardened violator of the laws of society, is not altogether without it." Smith believed that not all altruism was, or should be, reciprocally motivated, and sadly, it's not clear whether modern capitalists would compare favorably with the greatest ruffians and most hardened violators of his time.

Much of what is sold to us as essential to modern capitalism is not so. The problem isn't the "invisible hand."* It has delivered spectacular results, perhaps too

---

* *Itself almost invisible in Smith's writings, mentioned but three times in a million-plus words.*

Tongue hanging out like a man's tie
Spanish: to be exhausted

effectively. The problem is the invisible face of capital-ism. It face-less-ly separates the cooperating parties into emotionally isolated, inhuman, reluctant players of the game. The game wasn't intended to be, and needn't be, so amoral. It could be designed with more natural lim-its, more balance, and for greater overall benefit. Per-haps the invisible hand now needs a visible restraint to remind it of its connection to humanity.

Okay, enough of my rant on the follies of modern capitalism and the dangers of the unchecked puritanical work ethic.* Let's turn our attention to how we typically keep score in the *rat race*. I mean money, of course. Specifically, let's look at what the psychology of money tells us about the workings of our own minds.

I was overjoyed to hear that *homo economicus,* that paragon of rationality and utility maximization,** has been quietly put out of its, and more importantly, our, misery. Economists (though not Adam Smith) used to assume that we make our decisions hyper-rationally, driven primarily by self-interest. That assumption is baked into the modern view of capitalism. An accumulated mass of scientific evidence, however, tells us that classical economists are wrong about human nature. By nature, we are not built to be cold and calculating in our reasoning; nor are we designed to be only self-interested. These are among the worst errors of the Enlightenment. But we shouldn't have to look to the work of dismal scientists to tell us this. The primary empirical evidence of our own everyday lives should be more than enough to prove that human behavior is not rational.

In case you aren't convinced by your own life, here is a summary of my favorite experiment from behavioral economics that proves the point: the Ultimatum Game, which has a Proposer and a Responder. In the simplest

---

* H. L. Mencken's joyful definition of a Puritan: one who is fearful that someone, somewhere is happy.

** Utility maximization—Enron's initial business plan?

version, each has perfect information and plays a single game. The Proposer is given a sum of money; the Responder knows how much. The Proposer then has to offer the Responder *a piece of the pie*. The Responder can either accept or reject it. If the Responder accepts, each of the players gets a share and they both *go on their merry ways*. However, if the Responder rejects, neither gets to keep any of the money. Classical economics predicts that whatever is offered should be accepted. After all, the Responder is getting something for nothing, so accepting is the "rational" choice. However, that's not what happens. On average, the typical offer is less than half, in line with the homo economicus predictions. There is always a point, however, below which Responders behave in a way that doesn't fit the homo economicus model (i.e., supposedly "irrationally"). If the offer is considered too low, Responders reject. The prevailing opinion as to why this occurs is that Responders are viewing a low offer as being unfair or humiliating. In any case, by rejecting, Responders incur real costs (the foregone share) to punish Proposers. This study has been replicated many times in many cultures. It seems that we humans have a built-in mechanism telling us that we should disrupt a situation in which we feel unjustly treated—and that we should incur costs to enforce our preference for being treated justly.

Much other research has shown that evolution has equipped us to use our brains in ways that aren't simply what would be thought of as purely logical. The logic of survival of our deep ancestors hunting and gathering on the African savannah didn't equip us to be self-interestedly rational (to be modern-capitalist automata).

The Ultimatum Game also has confirmed that classical economists have been trying *to make monkeys of us* all. Scientists are trying to present animals with the closest thing they can come up with to economic choices. For monkeys, it's all about marshmallows or raisins. When simplified versions of the Ultimatum Game are run with chimpanzees, they always behave rationally.[7] *Chimpus economicus* is alive and well.

However illuminating, that isn't going to help with my bills, or, as the Italians say, "fine words don't feed a cat." So let's get back to the fine words of international idioms:

When we are *nose to the grindstone*, toiling Spaniards either "give callus" or "work at pure lung." Similarly, industrious Chinese work "with liver and brains spilled on the ground" and the equivalently conscientious Indian would have "no time to die." The French, when not working hard, also get lazy about their love of fine cuisine: They "gulp down flies." Italians are such a *bunch of mother's boys* that they call the person in charge "Mister sainted mother." To wield similar authority, a Spaniard requires a precise dress sense: He must "wear the pants well placed." A Japanese boss can exercise power by "using people with their chin."

If we are lucky, we have *deep pockets*. Similarly well-off Spaniards and Japanese have pockets that are cheerful and warm, respectively. For Frenchmen, to make lots of money is all about butter, either "making one's butter" or "putting butter in the spinach." We know which *side of our bread is buttered*. Hindi speakers need more; when well-off they prefer to have their "whole hand in the ghee/butter." Conversely, a poor English speaker might not have *two sticks to rub together*. An impoverished Hindi speaker doesn't "have a straw to use as a toothpick," which might not matter since the very poor also "have no tartar on their teeth." Meanwhile, a similarly strapped Japanese doesn't have any saliva—his "mouth dries up." Alternatively, an impecunious Japanese can be shameless; to be poor is to "become naked." Meanwhile, a needy Spaniard is worried about hygiene, being "cleaner than a frog's armpit."

INVOLVING WORK, WORKERS, MAKING AN HONEST LIVING

- A stink-of-sweat: *a workman (French)*
- A lead ass: *an office worker (French)*
- An ink sucker: *one who has a menial office job (Spanish)*
- Ink pisser: *an office worker (German)*
- A soup seller: *owner of a cheap restaurant (French)*
- A cow on casters or skates: *a traffic cop (French)*
- An art historian in civilian clothes: *a plainclothes agent (Russian)*

- A soul plumber: *a psychiatrist* * (German)
- Before God and the bus conductor we are all equal: *proverb (German)*
- No doctor is better than three: *proverb (German)*
- A young doctor makes a full graveyard: *proverb (China)*
- One who can be trusted: *a cook (Hindi)*
- The water business: *the entertainment business (Japanese)*
- Better to be a mouse in a cat's mouth than in a lawyer's hands: *proverb (Spanish)*

A NOT-SO-HONEST LIVING

- The gentleman on the roof beams: *thief (Chinese)*
- Shroud snatcher: *shameless thief (Hindi)*
- To hide between the fingers: *to steal (Hindi)*
- Not pure flour in the sack: *crook (Swedish)*
- One whose bow is drawn: *dangerous criminal (Hindi)*
- Steals the kohl [eyeliner] from the eye: *thief (Arabic)*
- To make long fingers: *to steal (German)*
- A hat burns on a thief: *a guilty conscience (Russian and Yiddish)*
- Word thief: *plagiarist (Hindi)*
- To connect one's blood vessels: *to conspire with (Japanese)*

* *In ancient Rome there was a job title called a* psychopompus—*a soul conductor. One of his duties was to poke fallen gladiators with a burning-hot metal rod to make sure they weren't faking. Also, many plumbers in ancient Rome were women.*

To crow
Spanish: to take advantage of financially

- A miller with hair on his teeth is honest: *proverb* (*German*)
- To suck juice: *to benefit at the expense of others* (*Japanese*)
- Criminal: *intelligent, well-done* (*Spanish, Puerto Rico*)
- To roll over while sleeping: *to dupe* (*Japanese*)

TO WORK HARD

- Sweat seven shirts: *work hard (Italian)*
- Too much meat on the fire: *overly busy (Italian)*
- Give callus: *work hard (Spanish)*
- Put a candle to it: *put some effort in (Spanish, Nicaragua)*
- Peel the garlic: *work like a dog (Spanish, Chile)*
- To a broken arm: *pushed to the limit (Spanish, Latin America)*
- At pure lung: *working hard (Spanish, Latin America)*
- With liver and brains spilled on the ground: *to do one's utmost (Chinese)*
- Wasteful with one's health: *burn the candle at both ends (German)*
- To have no time to die: *to be overwhelmed by work (Hindi)*
- Break a bone: *make a special effort (Japanese)*
- Make one's own body into powder: *worked to death (Japanese)*
- No time for a seat to get warm: *very busy (Japanese)*
- Break the horns: *work very hard (Spanish)*
- Dance on one's head: *work hard (Spanish)*
- To have moustaches: *a man of energy (Spanish, Latin America)*
- Get with one's own hump: *earn by one's own sweat (Russian)*

TO NOT WORK HARD

- To sell oil: *to goof off, to loaf (Japanese)*
- To not do a dry fig: *to be idle (Italian)*

To show your lamp to the sun
Hindi: to waste time, do something useless

- To make a worker's monument: *to be lazy (German)*
- Air man: *one with no work or income (Yiddish)*
- A codfish: *a lazy person (Spanish, Puerto Rico)*
- To gulp down flies: *to not work hard (French)*
- To make blue: *to take the day off (German)*

- A fan* in one's left hand: *an easy life with no work* (*Japanese*)
- By not wetting one's hands: *without any effort* (*Japanese*)
- To count stars: *to twiddle your thumbs* (*Russian*)
- To break [one's] chair: *to be very idle* (*Hindi*)

TO NOT WORK WELL OR NOT WORK ANYMORE

- To drown in a glass of water: *incompetent* (*Spanish*)
- To plough in the sea: *to do something useless* (*Spanish, Mexico*)
- To throw water into the sea: *to be useless* (*Spanish*)
- To be a piece of meat with eyes: *to be useless* (*Spanish*)
- A Buddhist priest for three days: *a quitter* (*Japanese*)
- To serve neither God nor the devil: *to be useless* (*Spanish, Mexico*)
- To be worth a mushroom: *to be worthless* (*Spanish, Chile*)
- To be worth potatoes: *to be worthless* (*Spanish, Mexico*)
- Not even to dress saints: *worthless* (*Spanish*)
- Poop on a stick: *worthless* (*Yiddish*)
- Thinner than water: *worthless* (*Hindi*)
- Ganges of dung: *a useless person, complete fool* (*Hindi*)
- He's good only for a fowl sacrifice: *useless* (*Yiddish*)
- Like a deaf man at a wedding party: *a useless person* (*Arabic*)
- Big shoe: *an incompetent person* (*Italian*)
- To comb the giraffe: *to waste effort* (*French*)
- To break firewood: *to waste effort* (*Russian*)
- To sift dust: *to waste effort* (*Hindi*)

---

* In ancient Rome the fan slave was called a flabelifier.

- Pedaling in yogurt: *ineffective (French)*
- To spread bean paste on something: *to make a mess (Japanese)*
- Too many saints ruin the temple: *too many cooks spoil the broth (Hindi)*
- The bath house soap bowl is missing: *chaos (Arabic)*
- Shoelace ironer: *too much attention to detail (Russian)*
- A pea counter: *one overly concerned with details (German)*
- A mouse milker: *one overly concerned with details (German)*
- Sewn with a hot needle: *done carelessly (German)*
- To show your lamp to the sun: *to waste time, do something useless (Hindi)*
- A poor dancer is impeded by his own balls: *a bad workman blames his tools (Russian)*
- For an unskilled dancer the courtyard is uneven: *a bad workman blames his tools (Hindi)*
- Painting little bars: *unemployed (Spanish, Colombia)*
- Reduced to a neck: *to be fired (Japanese)*
- To have to take a hat: *forced to resign (German)*
- Out to plant cabbage: *retired, old (French)*

TO INGRATIATE

- Foot licker: *a sycophant (Italian)*
- A sock sucker: *a sycophant (Spanish, Peru)*
- To lick someone's heels: *to behave in a servile manner toward someone (Russian)*

- Climb on the dragon and get close to the phoenix: *ingratiate oneself (Chinese)*
- To grind sesame: *to flatter (Japanese)*
- To pat over the wool: *to flatter, ingratiate (Russian)*
- Under the sleeve: *money under the table, a bribe (Japanese)*
- A silver shoe: *a bribe (Hindi)*

THE BOSS, THE MAN, THE WOMAN

- Armchair: *position of power (Italian)*
- Mister sainted mother: *the big boss (Italian)*
- The big head: *the boss (Italian)*
- To cut the cake: *to take control (Spanish, Chile)*
- To wear the pants well placed: *to impose authority (Spanish)*
- To tighten one's pants: *to make one's authority felt (Spanish, Costa Rica)*
- To have the frying pan by the handle: *to be in charge (Spanish)*
- To use someone with one's chin: *to order someone around (Japanese)*
- The rabbi's wife: *a pompous woman (Yiddish)*
- A company director's stomach: *a paunch (Japanese)*
- The eye of a typhoon: *a leading figure (Japanese)*
- A thick stick: *an important person, boss (Spanish, Chile)*
- A fat fish: *a big shot, head honcho (Spanish)*

POOR OR BROKE

- To be in the green: *to be broke (Italian)*
- Living by sheltering from the rain and dew:
  in poverty (Japanese)
- One's mouth dries up: *in poverty (Japanese)*
- To lack a straw for a toothpick: *not have a penny (Hindi)*
- No tartar on the teeth: *in poverty (Hindi)*
- An ant milker: *a miser (Arabic, Syrian)*
- Cleaner than a frog's armpit: *flat broke (Spanish)*
- To not have a single radish: *flat broke (French)*
- One who lives on watery lentils: *a poor person (Hindi)*
- Grass at a village site: *a poor man, easily trampled on (Hindi)*
- To drink a cup of broth: *to go broke (French)*
- One's legs stick out: *to exceed one's income (Japanese)*
- One's pocket is lonely: *short of money (Japanese)*
- One's pocket is cold: *short of money (Japanese)*
- To become naked: *to go broke (Japanese)*
- A wheel of fire: *in financial straits (Japanese)*
- To be duck: *to be broke (Spanish, Peru)*
- Iron rooster: *stingy person (Chinese)*
- Like a poor person's funeral: *quickly (Spanish, Colombia)*

CHEAP OR STINGY

- Fine words don't feed cats: *talk is cheap (Italian)*
- To have holes in your hands: *to be cheap (Italian)*

- To walk with one's elbows: *to be stingy (Spanish, Cuba)*
- To crow: *to take advantage of financially (Spanish, Argentina)*
- Goose: *a freeloader (Spanish, Colombia)*
- Not eat an egg so as to not waste the shell: *be miserly (Spanish, Mexico)*

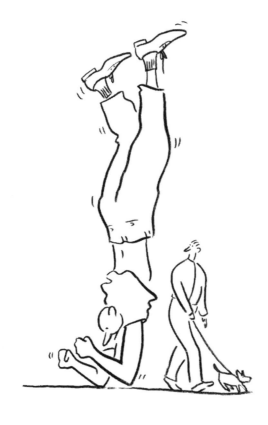

To walk with one's elbows
Spanish: cheap, stingy

To live on a large foot
German: to live very well

- Not eat a banana so as to not throw out the peel: *be miserly (Spanish, Mexico)*
- Worth a mushroom: *worthless (Spanish, Chile)*
- Worth potatoes: *worthless (Spanish, Mexico)*
- For an apple and an egg: *very cheaply (German)*
- A cucumber: *very cheaply (Hindi)*
- To light one's fingernail: *to lead a frugal life (Japanese)*
- To have a baby's hand: *to be very tight with money (Spanish, Chile)*
- To be hard of the elbow: *to be stingy (Spanish, Dominican Republic)*
- Eat vegetables and fear no creditors, rather than eat duck and hide: *proverb (Hebrew)*
- The painful one: *the check, bill (Spanish)*
- So cheap that she even farts inward: *extremely stingy (Finnish)*
- So miserly that if a fly fell in his tea, he would fish it out and suck it dry before throwing it away: *not an idiom, but a worthy inclusion, and all that in just two Hindi words! (Hindi)*

RICH/LUXURIOUS/GENEROUS

- To make one's butter: *to make lots of money (French)*
- To put butter in the spinach: *to improve one's living standard (French)*

- To cost the skin on one's buttocks: *to make a fast buck* (*French*)
- To have hay in your boots: *to feather your nest* (*French*)
- To have one's whole hand in the ghee [butter]: *to be wealthy* (*Hindi*)
- To have cheerful pockets: *to be wealthy* (*Spanish, Mexico*)
- One's pocket is warm: *wealthy* (*Japanese*)
- One's breast is deep: *generous* (*Japanese*)
- To live like God in France: *to live in luxury* (*German*)
- To live like a maggot in bacon: *to live in luxury* (*German*)
- To live on a large foot: *to live in luxury* (*German*)
- To earn oneself a golden nose: *to make a lot of money* (*German*)
- To have an elephant swing at the gate: *to live in luxury* (*Hindi*)
- To fly pigeons: *to have no cares, live in luxury* (*Hindi*)
- A wool sock well stuffed: *a nice nest egg* (*French*)
- Chickens do not peck the money: *to roll in money* (*Russian*)
- To be stuffed up, to be stuffed with: *to be very wealthy* (*Yiddish*)
- A rich man has no need of character: *proverb* (*Hebrew*)

TO SPEND MONEY

- To cost a candy: *expensive* (*French*)
- To cost an eye of the face: *expensive* (*Spanish*)

- Salty: *pricey, expensive (Spanish, South America)*
- To throw the house out the window: *to spend lavishly (Spanish)*
- Scratch the pocket: *spend reluctantly (Spanish)*
- The pure potato: *cold hard cash (Spanish, Colombia)*
- Despised metal: *money (Russian)*

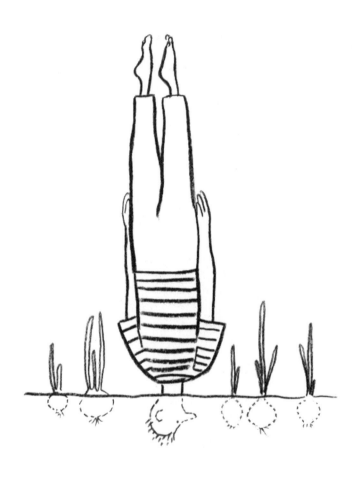

He should grow like an onion with his head in the ground.
Yiddish: go take a hike

chapter twelve

FOOD & DRINK

Give it to someone with cheese

MY PEOPLES WERE INVOLVED in a culinary coup d'état in 2001. It was a great year for Anglo-Indian food. Robin Cook, then the British Foreign Secretary, said in a speech that "chicken tikka masala is now a true British national dish, not only because it is the most popular, but because it is a perfect illustration of the way Britain absorbs and adapts external influences. Chicken tikka is an Indian dish. The masala sauce was added to satisfy the desire of British people to have their meat served in gravy."[1]

This momentous event addressed a couple of my food and identity issues. First, Britain isn't exactly respected for its national food. Non-Brits usually think of fish and chips and perhaps the full British breakfast (complete with black pudding—which is fried pig's blood sausage). So chicken tikka masala is a big step forward. Second, I'm a great consumer and promoter and provider of Indian food. I particularly enjoy breaking the bread of my ancestors with companions (at events known as Naan Nights). And the culinary influence of my ancestors isn't limited to Britain—one of Germany's most popular fast-food dishes is now the curry-wurst (more on Germans and their love of processed meats to follow).

As Robin Cook was pointing out, inclusion-and-fusion is a process often used by the British. It certainly applies to language as well as to food. Henry Hitchings, in his exuberant book *The Secret Life of Words,* estimates that English has added much flavor by gobbling up words from 350 other languages.[2] India has also practiced inclusion-and-fusion. I was a little shocked to discover that dishes we think of as characteristically Indian aren't entirely so. Curries rely on chilies that were brought to India by the Portuguese. Not a discovery that curried* favor with me.

Even the word *Indian* is of European origin. It was in use in England long before it was used in connection with the land of my ancestors. India originally meant any foreign land.[3] Hence it made sense, from a Eurocentric point of view, to speak of an East Indies and a West Indies, and to call the inhabitants of the Americas Indians. England and English are also so called for Eurocentric reasons. The word *England* is derived from the land of the Angles, who were a tribe of early invaders from what is present-day Germany and the northern Netherlands.

An idiom keeping alive an older meaning of curry—to groom or comb, as horses.

Getting back to food and national dishes …

For Italians we immediately think of pasta (though that is thought to have originated in China). Italians have particularly colorful language for their 500-plus varieties. Some of their entertaining translations include the familiar: worms (thin is *vermicelli* and thick is *vermicelloni*), little strings (*spaghetti*), spirals (*fusili;* same root as *fusilier,* or spiral), little tongues (*linguini,* or flattened spaghetti), knots of wood (*gnocchi*). But also the less familiar: little fingers (*ditalini*), little beards (*barbina*), moustaches (*mostaccioli*), little ears (*orecchiette*), half moons (*mezzalune*), pandas (*fantolioni*), butterflies (*farfalle*), infesting weed (*gramigna*), and, finally, the alarming priest chokers or strangled priests (*strozzapreti*)!

For the Japanese we think of sushi, though we often misconstrue that to mean raw fish. It actually refers to the fermented rice that the fish (or vegetables or meat) sits on. The Japanese take that rice very seriously. As Trevor Corson reveals in his delicious book *The Zen of Fish,* it can take a sushi chef in Japan up to two years just to learn how to get the rice right. American sushi chefs can learn *the whole shebang,* rice and all, in 12 weeks. Corson also reveals that sushi is like pasta, in that it probably originated in what is now part of China.

For the Spanish we think of paella and tapas. The word tapas means "lids" or "covers." Its use in relation to food supposedly derives from the practice of covering sherry glasses in Andalusia with thin slices of bread or meat to keep the flies off. A related recently invented word from The Daily Candy Lexicon is *crapas,* used to describe the terrible finger food served at public relations events.[4]

We've seen how language can provide a window into various ethnic stomachs. Let's see what other aspects of food culture idioms can shed light on:

For Germans, we perhaps think of their obsession with processed meats. While English speakers might be living *in the lap of luxury* or living the *life of Riley,* a similarly fortunate and content German prefers to be "living like a maggot in bacon." Processed meats also feature prominently in their expression for sulking, which is "to play the insulted liver sausage" and for "giving special treatment," which is "to fry a bologna sausage." Having given in too much to the temptations of their processed meats, dieting Germans can be described as engaging in the wonderfully graphic "de-baconing."

Though it is said that man cannot live by bread alone, she can use bread to ensure that she is not always alone. In English *we break bread with* friends (incidentally, that is what the word companion means: *com* ("with") + *pan* ("bread") = "bread fellow"). Similarly, social Russians "carry bread and salt" or "meet with bread and salt," and Arabs simply "take salt with you." And to further emphasize the perceived benefits of social eating, Arabs have a proverb that says, "An onion shared with a friend tastes like roast lamb."

Speaking of food, evolutionary psychologists have suggested that the absence of any effective form of refrigeration was critical to our early moral development. Let's say that you're an early humanoid hunting and gathering on the African savannah and you strike it lucky: You come across a huge beast and you manage to kill it. It yields far more meat than anyone involved in the hunt or their families can possibly consume. How do you get the most benefit of your excess meat without a fridge? Without anywhere to store it? The smartest of our deep ancestors would have stored their excess meat in the bodies and minds of others (not just their own kin). Provided those benefiting from your largesse could possibly repay your generosity in the future, that was the best thing you could do with excess meat. Groups of early humans who developed stable relationships and practiced this sort of reciprocal altruism were in a better position to prosper and multiply. Some of these adaptive benefits survive in our moral instincts today—even in forms of altruism that aren't so nakedly reciprocal. Refer, for example, to the earlier quotations from Adam Smith's first great work, *The Theory of Moral Sentiments* (see Chapter 11). Italians have a great word for gifts with strings attached that translates as "hairy generosity."

Speaking of food sufficiency, when we eat *to our heart's content,* Russians like "butter over the heart" and the Japanese more audibly "beat a belly drum." Meanwhile, "eating twice a day" is enough for Hindi speakers. For motivation, we can use a *carrot-and-stick* approach, but Germans express their preference for less nutritious incentives, requiring "sugar bread and whip." When we think that we are the *center of the universe* or the *bee's knees,* an equally egocentric Spaniard thinks she "is the hole in the center of the cake." And where we seek to *have our cake and eat it too,* the French prefer to "save the goat and the cabbage." Saving by "reheating the cabbage" for an Italian means dis-charmingly to attempt to revive a lapsed love affair. For the Dutch, to be enjoying good food is both sacred and grossly sacrilegious; it's like "an angel urinating on your tongue."

Along the lines of alcoholic associations, we think of Germany with beer, France with fine wines, Japan for sake, and Russia for vodka, any of which can lead to getting drunk. An inebriated Frenchman would be "buttered," a Spaniard "breast fed," a German could be either simply "blue," or perhaps "have a monkey sit on him." A not-so-great Dane might "have carpenters," implying that they were banging in his head. Italian idioms attest to the strength of the national relationship with coffee: Espresso is a "shrunken coffee," and liquor is "corrected coffee." As to the Italian understanding of corrected expectations, there is a proverb that warns, "You can't have a full barrel and a drunk wife."

Let's see what other enticing morsels of culinary culture are revealed by international idioms involving food.

COFFEE & TEA

- Shrunken coffee: *very strong espresso (Italian)*
- To do a java: *to have a party (French)*
- To brew the dirt from someone's fingernails and drink it: *to learn a bitter lesson from someone (Japanese)*
- A glass of warmth: *tea (Yiddish)*
- To make tea cloudy: *to dither (Japanese)*
- One's navel boils tea: *laughable (Japanese)*
- To bang on the tea kettle: *long-winded, annoying talk (Yiddish)*
- Don't stir the tea with your penis! (ouch): *Don't mess things up (Russian)*

ALCOHOL

- Good with the left hand: *to be a drinker (Japanese)*
- To have a glass up one's nose: *to have one too many (French)*
- To have a flag: *to reek of alcohol (German)*
- To buy oneself a monkey: *to get drunk (German)*
- Full of stars and hail: *very drunk (German)*
- To be buttered: *to be drunk (French)*
- To be breast-fed: *to be drunk (Spanish, Argentina)*
- To be blue: *to be drunk (German)*
- To have the canal full: *to be drunk (German)*
- To have a monkey sit on one: *to be drunk (German)*

To drown the mouse
Spanish: to take a drink to stave off a hangover

- To go along with one's cheek on the sidewalk: *to be drunk (Spanish, Mexico)*
- To have a guava tree: *to have a hangover (Spanish, Colombia)*
- To have a fat head: *to have a hangover (German)*
- The sound of cats mating: *to have a hangover (German)*
- To ferment one's wine: *to sleep off a hangover (French)*
- To have a mouth made of wood: *to have a hangover (French)*
- To drown the mouse: *to take a drink to stave off a hangover (Spanish)*
- A cask of wine has more miracles than a church full of saints: *proverb (Italy)*

HUNGRY

- Hungry like Virgin Mary: *starving (Italian)*
- To go with the long tooth: *dying of hunger (Spanish, Chile)*
- Bring the gut tied: *faint with hunger (Spanish, Mexico)*
- To be barking: *to be hungry (Spanish, Colombia)*
- Cleverer than hunger: *quick-witted (Spanish)*

EATING & OVEREATING

- Door hinge gobbler: *glutton (Spanish, Mexico)*
- To ring one's bell: *to feed one's face (French)*
- A good fork: *a hearty eater (Italian)*

- To do the little shoe: *to clean your plate (Italian)*
- The one of shame: *the last food on a plate that no one dares take (Spanish)*
- To beat a belly drum: *to eat heartily (Japanese)*
- To eat twice a day: *to have enough to eat (Hindi)*
- To undo twists in the entrails: *to eat one's fill after starving (Hindi)*
- Stomach fire: *indigestion (Hindi)*
- I already killed what was killing me: *I'm full (Spanish, Colombia)*

SALT

- To be salted: *to be unlucky (Spanish, Mexico)*
- Salty: *expensive (Spanish, South America)*
- With good salt and plums: *fortunately (Japanese)*
- Not allow salt in the soup: *grudgingly (German)*
- One eating salt: *servant or dependent (Hindi)*
- Faithlessness to one's salt: *ingratitude to a benefactor (Hindi)*
- We'll take salt with you: *acceptance of invitation to share a meal (Arabic)*
- To be like bread without salt: *bland, unattractive (Spanish, El Salvador)*
- To carry on like bread and salt: *to be good friends (Russian)*
- Meet with bread and salt: *warm welcome (Russian)*
- Like salt in flour: *plunged into difficulties (Hindi)*

- He is like salt: *someone who is into everything* (*Arabic*)
- A salty face: *a sullen face* (*Japanese*)
- To handle with salted hands: *to raise with tender care* (*Japanese*)
- To not have salt on the crown of the head: *not very bright* (*Spanish*)
- To put salt in the *kheer* [rice pudding]: *to ruin* (*Hindi*)

Stomach fire
Hindi: indigestion

SUGAR/CANDY/SWEETS/CAKES

- To cost a candy: *to be expensive (French)*
- To fix the cake: *to make amends (Spanish, South America)*
- What a bonbon, and me with diabetes!: *a street compliment (Spanish)*
- To cut the cake: *to take control (Spanish, Chile)*
- To be a caramel: *nice, a kind person (Spanish, Mexico)*
- To think one is the hole in the center of the cake: *to have a very high opinion of oneself (Spanish, Chile)*
- To pull through cocoa: *to ridicule (German)*
- Eat a drop of one's honey: *have a finger in the pie (Russian)*

BREAD

- To be as good as bread: *to be as good as gold (Italian)*
- To be better than bread: *to be as good as gold (Spanish)*
- To be like bread and cheese: *well-suited, well-matched (Italian)*
- To make a slice of bread and butter: *make a fuss (French)*
- Get your piece of bread: *one's comeuppance (Russian)*
- Tough piece of bread: *an old hand (Russian)*
- Sugar bread and whip: *carrot and stick (German)*
- To rely on bread and not eat cheese: *to be content with one thing (Spanish, Mexico)*

STARCHES/RICE/POTATOES

- To not know potato: *to know nothing (Spanish)*
- The pure potato: *cash (Spanish, El Salvador)*
- To not have even a potato: *to be broke (Spanish, Mexico)*
- To be in the potato: *to be in the money (Spanish, Panama)*
- Not a potato: *no joking matter (Russian)*
- To be a potato: *to be easy (Spanish, Chile)*
- Sweet potato-ed up: *a goofball (Spanish, Argentina)*
- Kasha in the mouth: *to mumble (Russian)*
- Has eaten little kasha: *is inexperienced (Russian)*
- Eat up your kasha: *get what's coming (Russian)*
- Walk around hot porridge: *beat about the bush (German)*
- To burn grilled rice cakes: *to be jealous (Japanese)*
- To eat cold rice: *to be in the doghouse (Japanese)*
- To eat bad-smelling rice: *to be in jail (Japanese)*
- You look like a clump of cooked rice: *you look stupid (Chinese)*
- To throw rice: *to criticize (Spanish, Peru)*
- To be like white rice: *to be everywhere (Spanish, Latin America)*
- We boil our rice only once: *proverb (India)*

CHEESE, BUTTER, & OTHER DAIRY

- To make a cheese: *to make a fuss (French)*
- To be the cheese on pasta: *to be perfect (Italian)*

- Give it to someone with cheese: *deceive or make fun of someone (Spanish)*
- Stick one's nose in every sour curd cheese: *be nosy (German)*
- To put butter in the spinach: *to improve one's living (French)*
- Like butter over the heart: *music to one's ears (Russian)*
- To have butter, money from butter, and the woman who made it: *to have it all (French)*
- To have the face of bad milk: *to look like one is in a bad mood (Spanish)*

EGGS

- Look for hairs inside an egg: *nitpick (Italian)*
- Go cook yourself an egg: *go fly a kite (French)*
- To not eat an egg so as to not waste the shell: *to be miserly (Spanish, Mexico)*
- Owl egg sunny-side up: *a practical joke (German)*
- To sit on eggs: *to be a recluse (Hindi)*

VEGETABLES

- Onion head: *someone with gray hair (Spanish, Mexico)*
- Onion seller: *overly sentimental (Spanish, Chile)*
- Onion tears: *crocodile tears, worthless tears (Yiddish)*

- He should grow like an onion: *with his head in the ground (Yiddish)*
- Onions should grow from your navel: *an insult (Yiddish)*
- To do the leek: *to hang around waiting (French)*
- To save the goat and the cabbage: *to have it all (French)*
- To be an asparagus: *to be skinny (French)*
- Go fry asparagus: *go fly a kite (Spanish)*
- Left in a fine eggplant patch: *in a mess (Spanish)*
- Simpler than a steamed turnip: *child's play (Russian)*
- Because of pure green peas: *for no reason (Spanish, Peru)*

Onions should grow from your navel
Yiddish: an insult

FRUITS

- What a fruit: *he is a rotten apple* (*Russian*)
- No place for an apple to fall: *no space* (*Russian*)
- Little mango: *good-looking person* (*Spanish, Latin America*)
- Ripe mango: *an ancient man or woman* (*Hindi*)
- To think one is the last suck on the mango: *to think highly of oneself* (*Spanish, South America*)
- Wind-fallen mangos: *something easy or cheap* (*Hindi*)
- A mango at the price of a stone: *a great deal* (*Hindi*)
- Have mangos and sell the seeds: *have it all* (*Hindi*)
- To not be a pear in sugar: *to be difficult* (*Spanish, Mexico*)
- To ask the elm tree for pears: *to ask in vain* (*Spanish*)
- To bring back one's strawberry: *to interrupt* (*French*)
- To have bad grape: *to be gruff* (*Spanish*)
- Big avocado: *bore, party pooper* (*Spanish, Puerto Rico*)
- Take your tomato: *get what you deserve* (*Spanish, Venezuela*)
- To go to the pineapple: *to fight* (*Spanish, Dominican Republic*)
- To be a coconut: *intelligent* (*Spanish, Latin America*)
- To give papaya: *something ridiculous* (*Spanish, Colombia*)
- Melon: *foolish, stupid* (*Spanish*)
- Apple of discord: *argumentative type* (*Spanish*)
- To sell like ripe cherries: *to sell like hot cakes* (*German*)
- Squeezer of limes: *a self-invited guest, an idler* (*Hindi*)

MEAT & FISH

- Wine and meat friends: *fair weather friends (Chinese)*
- To fry a bologna sausage: *to give special treatment (German)*
- When dogs were tied with sausages: *long ago (Spanish, Uruguay)*
- Roll as a sausage: *get lost (Russian)*
- A land of fish and rice: *a land of plenty (Chinese)*
- To smell the roast: *to be suspicious (German)*
- To eat owl's flesh: *to act foolishly (Hindi)*
- Dog cooker: *an outcast (Hindi)*
- Veal tenderness: *sloppy sentimentality (Russian)*
- A rubber eagle: *a tough roast chicken (German)*
- Meat in a kite's nest: *goes quickly, like hot cakes (Hindi)*

OTHER FOOD & DRINK-RELATED IDIOMS

- Like chewing sand: *unappetizing or dull food (Japanese)*
- He brings the mustard along: *he always has something to say (German)*
- Add oil and vinegar: *embellish a story (Chinese)*
- To matter a cumin seed: *to be unimportant (Spanish)*
- Carve out pretzels: *walk crookedly (Russian)*
- To give a drink from a coriander husk: *to tantalize (Hindi)*
- Soya bean paste: *insult (Japanese)*

By candlelight, a goat looks like a lady
French: look before you leap

chapter thirteen

FALSE FRIENDS

One's belly is thick

I T'S BAD ENOUGH THAT IDIOMS in their own languages aren't
easily understood. You have to be in the know in advance
to be able to substitute their intended meaning in your own
tongue. That's why idioms are the hardest things to learn
in another language. Translating idioms from another language often doesn't improve matters. A particularly mali-
cious subcategory of words and expressions are those which,
when translated, have a meaning that is very different in the
destination language to that intended in the source language.
These are known as *false friends*. You think you know them—
but that apparent familiarity breeds misunderstanding.

Speaking of falsity, variations of the Ultimatum Game,
which we met earlier (see pp. 189–190), can be used to keep
us honest. One of my favorite related quotes is from W. H.
Auden. He said that our commitment to the truth was the
"faintest of all human passions." Though we frequently
declare our interest in the truth, we just as frequently fail to
behave accordingly. Some Ultimatum Game variants include
information asymmetry. The Responder is *kept in the dark*

about the size of the pie. In this situation, Proposers tend to offer significantly less than half, which is an implicit lie about the size of the pie.

An experiment called the "Eyes of Honesty" is another great example of how non-conscious factors can affect the faintest of our human passions. It was carried out by Gilbert Roberts and two colleagues from the psychology department at Newcastle University in the U.K., where a coffee club operates on the honor system. Students are supposed to contribute every time they help themselves to a cup of coffee. To quote from the *New York Times*:[1]

"For 10 weeks ... [the researchers] alternately taped two posters over the coffee station. During one week, it was a picture of flowers; during the other, it was a pair of staring eyes....

A remarkable pattern emerged. During the weeks when the eyes poster stared down at the coffee station ... drinkers contributed 2.76 times as much money as in the weeks when flowers graced the wall [a 300% increase]. Apparently, the mere feeling of being watched—even by eyes that were patently not real—was enough to encourage people to behave honestly. Roberts says he was stunned: 'We kind of thought there might be a subtle effect. We weren't expecting such a large impact.'"

And I'm stunned also! Clearly, although everyone consciously knew the eye poster wasn't really watching, they couldn't help but be non-consciously affected.*

---

* H. L. Mencken defined conscience as the "inner voice that reminds you someone may be looking."

We can also be our own false friends. Ambrose Bierce, in his *Devil's Dictionary,* defines a *liar* as "a lawyer with a roving commission." That's an excellent summary of the role of our "inner lawyers," which is an expression used by Jonathan Haidt in his excellent *Happiness Hypothesis.* He uses *inner lawyer* to describe another cognitive bias that's baked into our minds. We rarely disinterestedly weigh all sides of a decision as we like to think we do. We usually operate with motivated reasoning. We frequently have a preference (often non-consciously arrived at) and send our inner lawyers off on a "one-sided search for supporting evidence." As soon as we have support for the answer we wanted, we stop gathering evidence, and we stop paying our inner lawyers. We all suffer from this confirmation bias. Haidt uses an underlying metaphor throughout his book to describe the relationship between our conscious and non-conscious minds. The former he thinks of as a monkey riding the latter, which is an elephant. In this case he says our elephants are not inquisitive clients for our inner lawyers.[2]

ANIMALS

- He's really a chicken: *easily fooled (Italian)*
- To die chicken: *to not reveal a secret (Spanish, Chilean)*
- A good duck: *a sucker (Japanese)*
- Pluck the turkey: *make love at a window (Spanish)*

Dog tail remains crooked
Arabic: a leopard doesn't change its spots

- Dog tail remains crooked: *a leopard doesn't change its spots* (*Arabic*)
- Female fox: *nasty, bitchy woman* (*Spanish*)
- To be made foxes: *to be in bad shape or badly dressed* (*Spanish*)
- Bull: *eunuch or impotent man* (*Hindi*)
- A cat defecates: *to pocket something stealthily* (*Japanese*)
- To set the dogs on someone: *to flirt* (*Spanish, Latin America*)
- To have some quality of a dog: *to be stylish* (*French*)
- Go to the dog house: *go to bed when very tired* (*Spanish*)
- To make music: *to complain* (*French*)
- To lay a rabbit: *to stand someone up* (*French*)
- To have eaten a monkey: *to be crazy about someone* (*German*)
- A fly on the nose: *a chip on the shoulder* (*Italian*)
- To undo a bear for someone: *to pull someone's leg* (*German*)
- To become a tiger: *roaring drunk* (*Japanese*)

COLORS

- To be in the green: *broke, poor* (*Italian*)
- A blue prince: *an ideal man* (*Spanish*)
- To make blue: *to take the day off* (*German*)
- To see nothing but blue: *to be in the dark, blissfully ignorant* (*French*)

- To be blue: *to be drunk, plastered (German)*
- To not be green: *to dislike (German)*
- Yellow: *green with envy (German)*

APPEARANCES

- One's belly is thick: *big hearted (Japanese)*
- To be tied up: *to be well turned out, very chic (French)*
- One's belly balloons: *to get frustrated from being quiet (Japanese)*
- Stick face: *person with a lot of nerve (Spanish, Chile)*
- To pull up the bottom of one's kimono and reveal the buttocks: *to maintain a defiant attitude (Japanese)*
- By candlelight, a goat looks like a lady: *look before you leap (French)*
- Square: *well built (Spanish)*
- To give someone a big head: *to bash someone's face (French)*

PEOPLE & PEOPLE PARTS

- To pull one's trousers down: *to surrender (Italian)*
- To bang your butt on the ground: *hysterically funny (French)*
- To stick one's chin out: *to become exhausted (Japanese)*
- To tighten one's belly: *to set one's mind (Japanese)*
- To scratch someone's back: *to outsmart someone (Japanese)*

To pull the hair from someone's nostril

Japanese: to dupe

- To take by the chin: *to caress, to appease (Hindi)*
- To put saliva on one's eyebrows: *to take with a grain of salt (Japanese)*
- To lower the outside corners of one's eyes: *to be pleased (Japanese)*
- To pull the hair from someone's nostril: *to dupe (Japanese)*
- To take off the nose ring: *to become a widow (Hindi)*

False Friends

To bite the moon
French: to try the impossible

- To be born in a shirt: *to be born with a silver spoon in one's mouth (Russian)*
- To produce wind at the corners of one's mouth: *to be eloquent (Chinese)*

- One's liver is extracted: *to be dumbfounded (Japanese)*
- To cure one's belly: *to get revenge (Japanese)*
- To grasp someone's tail: *to obtain evidence (Japanese)*
- From the view of the nose: *rule of thumb (French)*
- Butt is fringed with noodles: *to be very lucky (French)*

FOOD

- To throw rice: *to criticize (Spanish, Peru)*
- To peel the garlic: *to work like a dog (Spanish, Chile)*
- To cost a candy: *to cost an arm and a leg (French)*
- To eat twice a day: *to have enough to eat (Hindi)*
- To make a slice of bread and butter: *to make a fuss (French)*
- Squeezer of limes: *a self-invited guest, an idler (Hindi)*
- To fry a bologna sausage: *to give special treatment (German)*
- I'm not hanging noodles on your ears: *I'm not pulling your leg (Russian)*

ROMANCE

- To hang oneself: *to get married (Spanish, Mexico)*
- To give the package: *to stand up (Italian)*
- Oversized pants: *a man pushed around by his wife or girlfriend (Spanish)*

- To have fast hands: *a womanizer (Japanese)*
- To strike the four hundred blows: *to sow one's wild oats (French)*
- To leave someone nailed: *to dump someone (Spanish)*

MONEY & WORK

- Criminal: *intelligent; well done, extraordinary (Spanish, Puerto Rico)*
- The big head: *the boss (Italian)*
- Salty: *pricey (Spanish, South America)*
- To give [someone] time: *to fire someone (Japanese)*
- To count stars: *to twiddle your thumbs (Russian)*
- Big shoe: *incompetent (Italian)*
- To wear the pants well placed: *to impose one's authority (Spanish)*

ACTIVITIES

- To make music: *to complain (French)*
- To let off one's gun: *to have a great time (French)*
- To ring one's bell: *to eat (French)*
- To make wind: *to brag (German)*
- Give a greeting to the oldest woman in your house: *insult (Spanish, Mexico)*
- To put someone to sleep: *to deceive someone (Spanish, Mexico)*

- To go to open country: *to relieve oneself (Hindi)*
- To make an occasion white: *to spoil it (Italian)*
- To roll over while sleeping: *to double-cross someone (Japanese)*
- To look on over one's shoulder: *to look down on (German)*
- Window-licking: *window shopping (French)*
- Thumbs up: *illiterate (Hindi)*
- To bite the moon: *to try the impossible (French)*

Here the donkey falls
German: that's the important part

chapter fourteen

IN CONCLUSIVENESS

The end is musk

RESTLESS GRAVE-Y TRAIN OF THOUGHT

ORWELL WOULD THINK THIS A GRAVE turning of affairs, but Shakespeare would have approved. And though the following sentence might prevent further page turning, I'll ask you to grant me some platitude. I'll *wrap things up, by tying together some loose ends.*

In these concluding remarks, I'll speak up for idioms and their enduring popularity, and start to put idiom-ology onto a less infirm footing. Finally, I'll summarize the evidence we've seen, of how our minds are not what we'd like to think, and in doing so serve notice on Aristotle, Descartes, and all else who now unquestioningly serve the "hegemony of reason" that their time is up. The *scientifically correct* position is that we are not built to be dominated by the rational. It's time for us to wholeheartedly and wholemindedly embrace those elements of our nature that provide needed counterbalance to reason (and its cold rationality). It's time for all of us to Enlighten up!

LANGUAGE ORIGIN-OLOGY
The Jig Is Up

We've encountered several theories of language origin-ology ("la-la," "woo-woo," "poo-poo," "tut-tut"). The studious among you may have noticed that, although I've talked a lot about evolution in general, I've avoided using too many evolutionary terms when talking specifically about the origin and development of language. That's not out of pious *politically correct*-ed deference to the intelligent design demographic, but in *light of the fact* that the *scientifically correct* position isn't clear.

Very *big cheese* scientists have championed the view that language didn't evolve as a result of natural selection. They think it a glorious accident (so perhaps we could call that the "oops-wow" theory). The founder of modern linguistics, Noam Chomsky, is a prominent proponent. He has argued that language was an accidental by-product of other evolved changes, like our increase in cognitive capacity.[1] A good recent statement of this position is the paper Chomsky wrote with W. T. Finch and Marc Hauser, "The Faculty of Language: What Is It, Who Has It, and How Did It Evolve?" The late Stephen Jay Gould, himself a leading evolution scientist and best-selling science writer, called such by-products "spandrels." *Spandrel* is a term from architecture for a feature that isn't explicitly designed but that arises from the way other features fit together. The archetypal example of a spandrel is the space left between arches. Another term applied to these kinds of features is *exaptive.*

Other *big cheeses,* like Ray Jackendoff and Stephen Pinker, are solidly on the other side of this issue: They challenge the exaption-ists by taking the seemingly innocuous position that language is no different from any other complex feature or capability. The battle is unresolved ... and, looking at the language of its skirmishes, is illuminating. Plus it turns out that humble old idioms are proving to be not so humble after all. ...

Idioms Crucial in Scientific Cat Fight

A pivotal salvo in the language origin-ology battle was put forth by Jackendoff and Pinker in a paper called "The Nature of the Language Faculty and Its Implications for the Evolution of Language,"[2] published in response to the article by Finch, Hauser, and Chomsky. I don't need to go into all the details, but check out this point: "The key phenomenon is the ubiquity of idioms .... Speakers know, alongside their knowledge of words, an enormous number of idioms!"

One of the examples that Jackendoff and Pinker use is an idiom that also happens to be a complete sentence: *The jig is up.* Perhaps not coincidentally it also captures the gleeful tone of the authors who think they have incontrovertible evidence with which to support their case. The main point they are gloating over is that idioms are not insignificant peripheral oddities in language. Instead, idioms are a central feature, and they operate outside normal language rules and, in some cases, within those rules. That's what makes them useful in the debate. They violate the predictions of the oops-wowers. It seems that linguistics may have been too word-centric. The discipline has ignored the usefulness and popularity of idioms.

And to emphasize the *up-jig*-iness of the situation, Jackendoff and Pinker use a surprisingly (unscientific) tone: "It is only by omitting this ... alternative that Chomsky can maintain that nothing distinguishes the use of language for communication from the use of hair styles for communication." As the Japanese might say, that probably got the oops-wow-ers "anger hair pointing to heaven." Jackendoff and Pinker go on to say, "The assertion is that all hypotheses about adaptation are 'equally pointless'.... The argument seems to be that 'adaptive explanations can be done badly, so no one should ever attempt to do them well' ... evidently the charge of pointlessness is being wielded selectively." A reminder that the use of the scientific method doesn't preclude the use of unscientific and emotional language.

Leaving aside the nitty-gritty of the debate, idioms are of central importance to language!

IDIOM-OLOGY

On the Specious Origin of Idioms

Like all good evolution stories, the study of the origin of idioms depends on a careful look at the various species alive today and their relation to each other. It also depends on evidence gleaned from sifting through the remains of those long dead, i.e. on lexical archeology. Different degrees of deadness apply to the two main species of idioms described below.

Inadvertent Idioms: Debagging the Cat

Many idioms started out as *plain old* metaphors. Turns of phrase that required no turn of meaning, they were initially transparently understandable. We *let the cat out of the bag* as an example earlier. We no longer *buy pigs in pokes*—or in bags. And now we have more modern ways to *caveat emptor*. Cultural change and semantic drift loosened these expressions from their initial "moorings" and their meanings changed. Though it's very unlikely the change happened in *one fell swoop*. Drifting entirely away from their semantic anchors would have been a slow process. For example, the first recorded use of *one fell swoop* is in Shakespeare's *Macbeth. Fell* then meant "evil" or "ill-boding." He uses it to describe a kite, a small member of the hawk family. His audience would have understood that the swooping bird of prey was menacing. Often now we see the idiom morphing into *one foul swoop*. This is itself an example of how even the words in dead metaphors aren't entirely inactive.

Intentionally Opaque Idioms: Couch Potatoes

Many idioms started out opaque *from the get go*. As in-jokes that leaked out beyond the initial in-crowd. A great example of a whole *boat load* of these is Cockney rhyming slang. Cockneys, a community in the East End of London, are described by Bill Bryson in his engrossing *Mother Tongue* as among the most artful of English speakers.[3] To a Cockney *apples and pears*, *Adam and Eve,* and *trouble and strife* mean respectively "stairs," "believe," and "wife." As you can see, the second word of each expression rhymes with its intended meaning. For the following sentence, "Would you believe my wife can't get down the stairs?", a Cockney could say: "Would you Adam and Eve it, the trouble and strife can't get down the apples and pears?" Though they usually take it a step further to use only the first non-rhyming word, which would make that example sentence, "Would you Adam it, the trouble can't get down the apples?" Note that Cockneys are using some of Shakespeare's *functional shiftiness* to enliven their speech. Bryson also mentions the following as examples: loaf from loaf of bread = head; butcher from butcher's hook = look; china from china plate = mate, and tom from tomfoolery = jewelry.

For an example closer to home, let's look at how *couch potatoes* got so comfortably planted in our language. Alan Metcalf, in his great survey *Predicting New Words,* tells their tale, connecting a vegetative pun with an organized sect of sci-fried TV fans.[4] Their in-joke came from remote beginnings and has gotten entirely out of hand. Initially, a group of nine Californians religiously gathered to watch their favorite TV show, "Lost In Space." One of them punned from his love of TV-watching the verb "tubing," hence making them *tube*-ers. And, of course, potatoes are also tubers. The cult grew, its followers dedicated to *peace-of-mind-less-ness,* or, as they put it, "pursuit of inner peace through the prolonged viewing of television." That quotation is from the *Official Couch Potato Handbook.* Metcalf uses it and a few other happenstances to illustrate that, for an in-joke to be successful and to *have legs* enough to escape beyond the initiating group, some help is usually required. In this case, much marketing of related joke products and books.

Cognitive Couch Potato-ness

As Orwell complained, many idioms are hackneyed *old tropes*, banal bromides, trite platitudes, or stereotyped clichés. A look at the semantic roots of each of these related expressions is revealing.

Hackneyed comes from the term for a breed of horse developed in England for routine mundane tasks. Leading to the sense of being becoming banal and trite through overuse.

A trope, most often encountered in the expression *old trope,* means a figure of speech used in a nonliteral way. Trope initially meant a word or phrase used as an embellishment in the sung parts of a medieval liturgy. It's originally from the Latin for turn (*tropus*), and it now has a pejorative sense of a hackneyed old phrase.

A bromide has a sense that something so described is trite or banal. It comes from bromine, a pungent and poisonous gas. The gas was so called from the Greek *bromos,* meaning stench. Bromides are stereotypically stinking.

A platitude is a flat, dull, or trite remark, especially one that is uttered as if it were fresh or profound. It comes from the French for flat (*plat,* which also gives us the word plate).

A trite remark, like a hackneyed expression, is lacking in freshness or effectiveness because of constant use or excessive repetition. It comes from the Arabic "to be worn or rubbed down."

The clinchers, however, are the *cliché* and the *stereotype.* Both are terms from the world of printing. They directly connect economies of effort in printing with Orwell's insight into the economies of mental effort gained by the use of idioms and stock phrases.[5] Both a cliché and a stereotype are groups of words or letters that occurred so frequently that it was worth a printer preassembling them as one-piece blocks, rather than reconstructing them letter by letter each time. Idioms are literally clichés. And there's no need

for them to bow to the stereotypical pejorative conno-
tations. Idioms should be proud that they are so useful,
that it's worth storing them in our brains as prepack-
aged bundles of meaning. Which we do on the right
side, along with our taboo curses.

SCIENTIFICALLY CORRECT MIND-SET-FREE
Reasoning Against the Old Hegemony of Reason

Our minds aren't what we'd like to think. The way we
think about the way we think is no longer *scientifically
correct*. We've encountered lots of examples of errors in
our *frame of mind*. The best short summary of the *state
of the art* I've seen is from George Lakoff, the leading
cognitive linguist (and metaphor-ician). He believes
that too much of our current thinking is based on the
erroneous metaphors of ancient Greeks (Aristotelian
radiators), disembodied reason-ers like Descartes, and
much else from the Enlightenment. The 18th-century
mind-set we've inherited is that reason is conscious,
literal, logical, universal, unemotional, disembodied, and built to serve our self-interest. Much of that
now doesn't match well with scientific data. It seems
our minds are too made up. Relying on the scientific
method (also a *brainchild* of the Enlightenment), we
now have a substantial *body of evidence* to counter the
"hegemony of reason."

Hairy Ancestors & Unhairy Generosity

The baked-in survival lessons of the fittest and sexiest of our deep ancestors didn't equip us to be Old Enlightenment thinkers. To take just a couple of examples: Our minds (and bodies) are built to do a lot of reasoning non-consciously. Perhaps as much as 90 percent of our information processing happens that way. The survival of the fastest-reacting early humans has ensured that we use our conscious minds only when it's already safe, and when we can afford the extra time it takes to give something deliberate thought. The prospering of the most sensibly cooperative ancient meat sharers has predisposed us to generosity (and not always as the Italians would say–the reciprocally "hairy" kind). The thrival of our most emotionally attuned face-reading fore-parents has left us with many traits that bind us psychobiologically to the well-being of others. We aren't built to be mainly self-interested; we have other-interest deep in our DNA. And that is one of the key reasons we should dethrone the Enlightenment mindset. Against our nature, self-interest has been given too high a moral priority.

Our Minds Were Mostly Made Up a Long Time Ago

Our best current science tells us that we are *at least of two minds*. We do have an 18th-century Englightenment reasoning part of our brains. It is slow, operates serially (attending to one thing at a time), and is conscious, consciously controllable, effortful, and dispassionate (cold and calculating). However, our minds are made up of more than just that. We also think quickly (we often react "without thinking"), in parallel, non-consciously, in ways beyond our control, effortlessly, and emotionally. Emotions are not the polar opposite of reason. We could think of them as habits of thought (of information processing) that were so useful and so important that we have circuits for them baked into the non-conscious layers of our minds (and bodies). We are built to use our emotions to guide our conscious reasoning. David Hume, the 18th-century Scottish anti-rationalist philosopher, knew this when he wrote that reason is, and ought only to be, the slave of the passions.

Enlighten Up!

Lakoff sums up the gaps between science and our 18th-century view of mind by calling for a New Enlightenment. Using the tools of the first Enlightenment we can improve our scientific and philosophical understanding of ourselves. The *scientifically correct* now need to join forces with humor's longstanding position as a weighty counter to the "hegemony of reason."[6] Plato understood the value of such an alliance; in condoning the use of comedy in his ideal state, he said, "For it is impossible to know serious things without becoming acquainted with the ridiculous."

ASSORTED HIND THOUGHTS
Play-gerism & Recycling

Paraphrasing Clive James in his astonishing encyclopedia of erudition, *Cultural Amnesia*, false wit consists in quoting from old books.[7] I am guilty of much quoting of others' wit (play-gerism). I hope, however, I can be considered less guilty in that I have included quotes from new books also. Another way to *vice-a-virtue* this—is that it's carbon friendly. Much of the wit herein is post-consumer recycled.

On Writing as Combat

Judith Thurman, in her wonderful collection of essays *Cleopatra's Nose* (so entitled because of Pascal's joke about how if hers had been shorter, the whole face of history would have been different), describes her experience of writing as "line by line combat." I wouldn't dream of putting this meager effort in the same ballpark as hers. But her thought now comes to my attention-deficient disorder-ly mind. Having now attempted to write, it seems my process has been a thought by thought, word by word, phrase by phrase struggle. And that's before getting to the lines ... I am now in even greater awe of real writers.

On Reading, Puns, & Lenient Sentencing

The pun has gotten a very bad rap. It is not the lowest form of wit. Some puns are low cringe-worthy crimes against humor. But many others serve a higher purpose.

They are not all just double entendres. My deep ancestors included elaborate punning in the highest of their literary forms. Sanskrit, like English, had an embarrassment of semantic riches. It could be written to incorporate and play on multiple meanings. So that a given sentence or passage could be read to have more than one parallel interpretation. Such poetry was designed to be read and savored in more than one pass. Inspired by my poetic ancestors, I whole-mindedly condone multiple meanings that conspire, with conviction, to serve the same sentence.

On Conversing

Clive James, whose wit I have already borrowed, said, "A writer leaves you everything to say. It is in the nature of the medium to start a conversation within you...." Since I'm not a writer, and certainly not in the sense James meant, it's *a tall order* to hope that something in these pages started a conversation in you. Still, perhaps one of the idioms in these pages will help you start a fruitful conversation with someone else. Perhaps this gathering of words can rise to the level of small-talk-provoking material, suitable for cocktail party chatter.

On Finifugal and Fini-frugal Gratitude

I dislike endings, but can't let this one pass without a brief word of gratitude. Thank you for sharing some of your limited and precious time. I hope it has been at least a pleasant pastime (or "thought expeller").

NOTES

INTRODUCTION

1. Ellen Bialystok, Fergus I. M. Craik, Morris Freedman, "Bilingualism as a Protection Against the Onset of Symptoms of Dementia," *Neuropsychologia* 45 (2007), 459–64.

2. Vicki Leon, *Working IX to V* (New York: Walker and Co., 2007), 90.

3. Nicholas Ostler, *Empires of the Word: A Language History of the World* (New York: HarperCollins, 2005), 545.

4. PBS broadcast. "Charlie Rose," October 28, 2008.

5. Clive James, *Cultural Amnesia: Necessary Memories from History and the Arts* (New York: W.W. Norton, 2007), 390.

6. Daniel Goleman, "Friends for Life: An Emerging Biology of Emotional Healing Essay," www.newyorktimes.com, October 10, 2006.

7. Stephen Pinker, *The Stuff of Thought: Language as a Window into Human Nature* (London: Penguin Books, 2007), 131.

8. William Safire, *The Right Word in the Right Place at the Right Time: Wit and Wisdom from the Popular Language Column in the New York Times Magazine* (New York: Simon & Schuster, 2004), 260.

9. Geoffrey K. Pullum, *The Great Eskimo Vocabulary Hoax and Other Irreverent Essays on the Study of Language* (Chicago: University of Chicago Press, 1991), 159.

10. Nicholas Kristof, "Our Racist, Sexist Selves," *New York Times,* April 6, 2008.

11. Safire, *The Right Word in the Right Place at the Right Time,* 159.

12. George Lakoff, *The Political Mind: Why You Can't Understand 21st-Century American Politics with an 18th-Century Brain* (New York: Viking, 2008), 232.

13. John Bargh, John H., Mark Chen, Lara Burrows, "Automaticity of Social Behaviour: Direct Effects of Trait Construct and Stereotype Activation on Action," *Journal of Personality and Social Psychology* 71 (1996), 230–244; as reported in Gary Kluge, *The Haphazard Construction of the Human Mind* (Boston: Houghton Mifflin, 2008), 25.

CHAPTER 1

1. Mark Liberman, "Darwin and Deacon on Love and Language," February 14, 2004. Available at http://itre.cis.upenn.edu/~myl/languagelog/archives/000453.html; or Charles Darwin (1871; 2nd ed. 1879), *The Descent of Man, and Selection in Relation to Sex.*

2. Geoffrey Miller, *The Mating Mind: How Sexual Choice Shaped the Evolution of Human Nature* (New York: Random House, 2001).

3. C. D. Ankney, "Sex Differences in Relative Brain Size: The Mismeasure of Woman, Too?" *Intelligence* 16, 3–4 (1992), 329–36.

4. Jennifer Conellan, Simon Baron-Cohen, Sally Wheelwright et al., "Sex Differences in Human Neonatal Social Perception," *Infant Behavior and Development* 23 (2001), 113–18.

CHAPTER 2

1. Howard Rheingold, *They Have a Word for It* (Tarcher, 1988), 90.

2. Angela Friederici, Manuela Friedrich, Anne Christophe, "Brain Responses in 4-month-old Infants Are Already Language Specific, *Current Biology* 17:17 (14), July 2007, 1208-11.

3. Barbara Wallraff, *Word Fugitives: In Pursuit of Wanted Words.* (New York, HarperCollins, 2006), 4.

4. Roy Blount, Jr., *Alphabet Juice: The Energies, Gists, and Spirits of Letters, Words and Combinations Thereof* (New York: Farrar, Straus and Giroux, 2008), 98.

5. Safire, *The Right Word in the Right Place at the Right Time,* 296.

6. Cabinet Magazine and David Greenberg, *Presidential Doodles: Two Centuries of Scribbles, Scratches, Squiggles, and Scrawls from the Oval Office* (New York: Basic Books, 2007), 199.

7. Jonathan Haidt, *The Happiness Hypothesis: Finding Modern Truth in Ancient Wisdom* (New York: Basic Books, 2006), 54.

CHAPTER 3

1. Christine Kenneally, *The First Word: The Search for the Origins of Language* (New York: Viking/Penguin, 2007).
2. Benedict Carey, "Alex, a Parrot Who Had a Way With Words, Dies," www.newyorktimes.com, September 10, 2007.
3. Kenneally, *The First Word*, 95.
4. Miller, *The Mating Mind*, 54.
5. Jonah Lehrer, *Proust Was a Neuroscientist* (Boston: Houghton Mifflin, 2007), 69–70.

CHAPTER 4

1. Nicholas Kristof, "Our Racist, Sexist Selves."
2. Martin Seligman, *Authentic Happiness. Using the New Positive Psychology to Realize Your Potential for Lasting Fulfillment* (New York: Free Press, 2004), 5.
3. Richard Wiseman, *Quirkology: How We Discover the Big Truths in Small Things* (New York: Basic Books, 2007), 176.

CHAPTER 5

1. Tom M. Mitchell, Svetlana V. Shinkareva, Andrew Carlson et al., "Predicting Human Brain Activity Associated with the Meanings of Nouns," *Science* 320 (2008), 1191–95.
2. "Scientists Watch as Listener's Brain Predicts Speakers' Words," *Science News Daily,* September 15, 2008.

3. Philip Davis, *Shakespeare Thinking* (London, New York: Continuum), 92.

4. Philip Davis, "The Shakespeared Brain," *The Reader* 23 (2006), 39–43.

5. M. Oliveri, L. Romero, C. Papagno, "Left But not Right Temporal Involvement in Opaque Idiom Comprehension: A Repetitive Transcranial Magnetic Stimulation Study," *Journal of Cognitive Neuroscience* 16 (2004), 848–55; Monica-Zita Zempleni, Marco Haverkort, Remco Renken, "Evidence for Bilateral Involvement in Idiom Comprehension: an fMRI Study," *NeuroImage* 34 (2006), 1280–91; Leonor J. Romero Lauro, Marco Tettamanti, Stefano F. Cappa et al., "Idiom Comprehension: A Prefrontal Task?" *Cerebral Cortex* 18 (2008), 162–70.

6. Maryanne Wolf, *Proust and the Squid: The Story and Science of the Reading Brain* (New York: HarperCollins, 2007), 3, 5.

CHAPTER 6

1. Henry Hitchings, *The Secret Life of Words* (New York: Farrar, Straus, and Giroux, 2008), 136, 137.

2. David Crystal, *Words, Words, Words* (New York: Oxford University Press, 2006), 59.

3. Bill Bryson, *The Mother Tongue: English and How It Got That Way* (New York: William Morrow, 1991), 13.

4. Ostler, *Empires of the Word*, 557.

5. Howard Rheingold, *They Have a Word for It*, 67.

CHAPTER 7

1. "Language Without Numbers: Amazonian Tribe Has No Word to Express 'One,' Other Numbers," *Science News Daily,* July 15, 2008.
2. Jim Holt, "Numbers Guy," *The New Yorker,* March 3, 2008.
3. Ibid.
4. Pinker, *The Stuff of Thought,* 114.
5. Michael S. Gazzaniga, *Human: The Science Behind What Makes Us Unique* (New York: HarperCollins, Ecco, 2008), 96.
6. Ibid., 96.

CHAPTER 8

1. Jack Hitt, "Say No More," www.newyorktimes.com, February 29, 2004.
2. Charles Darwin, *Physiognomy. Constitution of Man,* Number IX (1874).
3. Lehrer, *Proust Was a Neuroscientist,* 77–88.
4. Pinker, *The Stuff of Thought,* 195.
5. Ammon Shea, *Reading the OED: One Man, One Year, 21,730 Pages* (Perigee Trade, 2008).

CHAPTER 9

1. "How Grue Is Your Valley?" www.economist.com, January 18, 2007.

2. Roxanne Khamsi, "Russian Speakers Get the Blues," www. newscientist.com, May 1, 2007.

3. A. Franklin, G. V. Drivonikou, L. Bevis, "Categorical Perception of Color Is Lateralized to the Right Hemisphere in Infants, but to the Left Hemisphere in Adults," *Proceedings of the National Academy of Sciences*, USA 105 (2008), 3221–25.

4. Jim Holt, *Stop Me if You've Heard This: A History and Philosophy of Jokes* (New York: W.W. Norton, 2008), 104.

5. "All of Orwell," *The New Yorker*, 1946; reprinted in Clive James, *As of This Writing: The Essential Essays 1968–2002* (New York: W.W. Norton, 2003), 284.

6. Christopher Hitchens, *Why Orwell Matters* (New York: Basic Books, 2002), 11.

7. George Orwell, "Politics and the English Language, *Horizon–GB,* April 1946; reprinted in George Orwell, *Why I Write* (London: Penguin Books, 2004), 102.

CHAPTER 10

1. Malcolm Gladwell, *Blink: The Power of Thinking Without Thinking* (New York: Little, Brown, 2005), 197–212.

2. Stephen Pinker, "Holy @&%*!", *Wired Magazine*, August 21. 2007.

3. Pinker, *The Stuff of Thought,* 334.

CHAPTER 11

1. Douglas Caldwell, "University Panel Discussion on the Nature of Work in the United States," *Sacramento Business Journal,* February 28, 2003.
2. Lehrer, *Proust Was a Neuroscientist,* 76.
3. P. J. O'Rourke, *On The Wealth of Nations* (New York: Grove/Atlantic, 2006), 36.
4. Ibid., 198.
5. James Buchan, *The Authentic Adam Smith: His Life and Ideas,* (New York: W.W. Norton, 2006), 10.
6. Ibid., 56.
7. Keith Jensen, Josep Call, Michael Tomasello, "Chimpanzees Are Rational Maximizers in an Ultimatum Game," *Science* 316 (2007), 107–109.

CHAPTER 12

1. Robin Cook, "Robin Cook's Chicken Tikka Masala Speech," *The Guardian,* April 20, 2001.
2. Hitchings, *The Secret Life of Words,* 144.
3. Ibid.
4. Editors, *The DailyCandy Lexicon: Words That Don't Exist but Should* (Virgin Books, 2008), 43.

CHAPTER 13

1. Clive Thompson, "The Eyes of Honesty," www.newyork

times.com, December 10, 2006.

2. Haidt, *The Happiness Hypothesis,* 64.

CHAPTER 14

1. W. T. Fitch, M. D. Hauser, N. Chomsky, "The Evolution of the Language Faculty: Clarifications and Implications," *Cognition* 97 (2005), 179–210.

2. Ray Jackendoff, Stephen Pinker, "The Nature of the Language Faculty and Its Implications for the Evolution of Language," *Cognition* 97 (2005), 211–25.

3. Bill Bryson, *The Mother Tongue,* 236.

4. Alan Metcalf, *Predicting New Words* (New York: Houghton Mifflin, 2004), 129–33.

5. "All of Orwell," reprinted in James, *As of This Writing,* 284.

6. Lakoff, *The Political Mind.*

7. Clive James, *Cultural Amnesia: Necessary Memories from History and the Arts* (New York: W.W. Norton, 2008), 389.

REFERENCE SOURCES

Akiyama, Nobuo, and Carol Akiyama. *2001 Japanese and English Idioms*. Barron's Educational Series, 1996.

Albanese, Nicholas, Giovanni Spani, Phillip Balma, and Ermanno Conti. *Streetwise Italian Dictionary Thesaurus, The User Friendly Guide to Italian Slang and Idioms*. McGraw Hill, 2005.

Arany-Makkai, Agnes. *2001 Russian and English Idioms*. Barron's Educational Series, 1997.

Crystal, David. *As They Say in Zanzibar*. Oxford University Press, 2008.

Emmes, Yetta. *Drek! The Real Yiddish Your Bubbe Never Taught You*. Plume, 1998.

Kogos, Fred. *A Dictionary of Yiddish Slang & Idioms*. Citadel Press, 1998.

Lin, Marjorie, and Leonard Schalk. *Dictionary of 1000 Chinese Idioms*. Hippocrene Books, 2000.

McGregor, R. S. *Oxford Hindi-English Dictionary*. Oxford University Press, 1993.

McLoughlin, Leslie J. *A Learners Dictionary of Arabic Colloquial Idioms, Arabic-English*. Packard Publishing Ltd., 1998.

McVey Gill, Mary, and Brenda Wegmann. *Streetwise Spanish Dictionary/Thesaurus, The User Friendly Guide to Spanish Slang and Idioms*. McGraw Hill, 2001.

Pickup, Ian, and Rod Hares. *Streetwise French Dictionary/Thesaurus, The User Friendly Guide to French Slang and Idioms*. McGraw Hill, 2002.

Strutz, Henry. *2001 German and English Idioms*. Barron's Educational Series, 1995.

Vanderplank, Dr. Robert. *Uglier Than a Monkey's Armpit*. Boxtree, 2007.

REFERENCE SAUCES

The source of much flavor herein:

Bierce, Ambrose. *The Unabridged Devil's Dictionary.* University of Georgia Press, 2002.

Blount, Roy, Jr. *Alphabet Juice.* Farrar, Straus and Giroux, 2008.

Bryson, Bill. *The Mother Tongue.* Harper, 1991.

Buchan, James. *The Authentic Adam Smith.* Atlas, 2007.

Cabinet, David. *Presidential Doodles.* Perseus Books, 2006.

Corson, Trevor. *The Zen of Fish.* HarperCollins, 2007.

Crystal, David. *Language Play.* University of Chicago, 2001.

———. *Words Words Words.* Oxford University Press, 2007.

DailyCandy. *The DailyCandy Lexicon: Words That Don't Exist But Should.* Virgin Books, 2008.

Davis, Philip. *Shakespeare Thinking.* Continuum, 2007.

Dickson, Paul. *Family Words.* Marion Street Press, 2007.

Gazzaniga, Michael S. *Human, the Science Behind What Makes Us Unique.* Ecco, 2008.

Gladwell, Malcolm. *Blink.* Little Brown and Co., 2005.

Haidt, Jonathan. *Happiness Hypothesis.* Basic Books, 2006.

Hitchens, Christopher. *Why Orwell Matters*. Basic Books, 2003.

Hitchings, Henry. *The Secret Life of Words*. Farrar, Straus, and Giroux, 2008.

Holt, Jim. *Stop Me if You've Heard This*. W. W. Norton, 2008.

James, Clive. *As of This Writing*. W. W. Norton, 2003.

———. *Cultural Amnesia: Necessary Memory from History and the Arts*. W. W. Norton, 2008.

Kenneally, Christine. *The First Word*. Viking, 2007.

Lakoff, George. *The Political Mind*. Viking, 2008.

Lehrer, Jonah. *Proust was a Neuroscientist*. Houghton Mifflin, 2007.

Leon, Vicki. *Working IX to V*. Walker and Company, 2007.

Marcus, Gary. *Kluge*. Houghton Mifflin, 2008.

McWhorter, John. *Word on the Street*. Basic Books, 2001.

Metcalf, Allan. *Predicting New Words*. Houghton Mifflin, 2004.

O'Rourke, P. J. *On The Wealth of Nations*. Grove, 2007.

Orwell, George. *Why I Write*. Penguin Classics, 2005.

Ostler, Nicholas. *Empires of the Word*. Harper, 2006.

Pinker, Stephen. *The Stuff of Thought*. Viking, 2007.

Safire, William. *The Right Word in the Right Place at the Right Time*. Simon & Schuster, 2004.

Seligman, Martin. *Authentic Happiness*. Free Press, 2004.

Shea, Ammon. *Reading the OED*. Perigee Trade, 2008.

Steinmetz, Sol. *Semantics Antics*. Random House, 2008.

Wallraff, Barbara. *Word Court*. Harcourt, 2000.

———. *Word Fugitives*. Collins, 2006.

Wiseman, Richard. *Quirkology*. Basic Books, 2007.

Wolf, Maryanne. *Proust and the Squid*. HarperCollins, 2007.

ACKNOWLEDGMENTS

I AM IMMEASURABLY INDEBTED to multitudes of contributors, without whom this book would not have been possible; including those who were unwittingly involved in creating the source (and sauce) references. Not to mention the untold millions whose distilled wit, wisdom, and linguistic innovation are reproduced herein. Also to those instrumental in the mechanics of this publication, including especially my editor, Barbara Noe, who in addition to being wonderfully professional, also had faith in the idea enough to get it to the right deciders. Her reward for this favoUr* was to be sentenced to make it happen; a process that included shepherding the highly disorganized material of an easily irritable author. My gratitude also goes to Melissa Farris, the artful book designer, and Julia Suits, the talented illustrator and *New Yorker* cartoonist, whose work enlivens, whimsifies, and adds juice to what could otherwise have been a dry text.

---

* Not a misspelling, this is a symptom of Irritable Vowel Syndrome, an irrational nostalgia for English English spellings that causes intermittent inflammation of irritatingly omitted vowels.

Additional thanks to assorted others who have contributed variously, including encouragement, ideas, jokes, time, detailed comments, flippant feedback, retorts, ridicule, and other forms of support: Michelle Yenchochic (of Diversified Reporting), Ama Wertz, Marco Robert, Bahar Salimova, Eric Roston, Jeremy Pietron, Bill Wright, Aparna Jain, Monty & Melissa & Asher Oppenheim, Tanya Yudelman Block, Nora Malikin, Eugenia Sidereas, and Louise & Nigel & Ida & Saga Biggar.

My thanks also to various running mates at Potomac Runners (led by the irrepressible Philip Davis), Perk-Uppers (including Devry Boughner, Justine and Rob Donahue, Tracy Wilson, Jennifer Eliot, and Denise and Bryan King), and Fleet Feet DC (led by the indefatigable Phil Fenty), who all facilitated a sociable sweat-soaked semblance of sanity.

Finally, to innumerable Knaan Knights and companions, who have broken the bread of my ancestors with me.

ABOUT THE AUTHOR

J AG BHALLA is an amateur idiomologist, amateur trivi-
ologist, amateur natural scientist, amateur entrepreneur,
amateur film producer, and now amateur author.

ABOUT THE ILLUSTRATOR

JULIA SUITS is a *New Yorker* cartoonist, painter, and geeky pursuer of the odd and overlooked.